MW00476756

Copyright © 2021 Doug Austin
All rights reserved.

CONTENTS

FOREWORD

This whole thing started when I was still in college. Actually it goes back further than that, more like middle school. You see I had this idea that if I could be Don Quixote that would be fantastic, the only trouble was I really wanted to drive a Porsche, not ride a donkey (and be a bit less crazy). So I quickly gave up on that idea and settled on being more in the idea business. That's when it all started, the notion of being an Ad Man (or at least that's how I thought of it at the time) would be my future and focus.

Fast forward to my senior year in college at Stephen F. Austin State University in Nacogdoches Texas, where I took an internship at my first agency. I honestly can't remember the name of the agency or even the players, but what I can remember is that this seemed like a lot of fun and something I really did think I would have a good time doing for the rest of my career. Upon graduation I sold everything I had worth anything and put it all towards getting my start in NYC. I got a haircut, bought a suit and on January 2, 1987 purchased a one-way, red-eye ticket to New York City.

I had one interview lined up that day with Marty Mitchell at Sawden and Bess advertising agency. You see Marty was a family friend and my mother had secured this introduction while she was back East on a visit with friends earlier that past fall. So, upon arrival in the city early that morning of January 3, I made my way to Grand Central Station and did the best I could to clean up in the public bathroom, fixed my tie and made my way to 52nd St. and Madison Avenue where Sawden and Bess was located. Marty was kind as he shook my hand and said "Welcome to the city, kid, what do you want to do?" I must've seemed pretty animated and excited because I literally sat two inches taller in my seat and said "I want to be in advertising — that's why I'm here." After a short round of interrogation it was decided that I would be in account services, as opposed to creative or media. I said that sounded great. Marty let me know that they didn't have any jobs, but account services is where I should look. Feeling a little discouraged, and a lot desperate, I asked Marty if he had any internships I could fulfill while I was looking around town. Marty let me know that they didn't have any internships. Feeling truly desperate now, and to be honest a little frantic, I had one last thought, which was to offer myself up for free, and that's exactly what I did. So, on that day, Marty, being the shrewd New York City Ad Man that he was, accepted my offer. My only request was that if I did a good job during my internship, he write me a letter of recommendation. Marty seemed to think that was a pretty good deal and agreed. He walked me down the hall and introduced me to a woman, maybe two years older than me, and said "This is your new boss, Gwen. Do a good job." And that was it. That was how I began my career in advertising as a free intern in New York City on January 3rd, 1987.

The story does not really end there if I'm honest. The full measure of my start in advertising in New York City really extends forward for three months as I began to interview and talk with the big city shops about entry level positions, which were very difficult to secure. You see, if you were from one of the Ivy League schools you had a leg up. I, being from Nacogdoches, Texas and Stephen F. Austin State University, had really no leg to stand on at all. But I was not deterred and went on many interviews and worked hard at Sawden and Bess where apparently they thought I did a good job as well. The end of my money was drawing near and the train pass I had in from Connecticut where I was staying, was going to run out in two weeks. If I didn't find a job during those two weeks, I was going back to Texas. I was going to be a bartender. I was pretty good at it and figured that would be fine. It occurred to me that I better check in with the big boss, Marty Mitchell, and see if any jobs had opened up. So one day, a little before lunch, I stopped in to see Marty. Marty told me he'd check on things and let me know. It seems he checked with Gwen and she said I had been doing a pretty good job. He also let me know that they were going to hire an assistant account executive for Gwen. When I heard this I got really excited, stood right up and I said "Hire me, I've been doing the work, I know what to do and I'm here already." I wish I could remember what the look on Marty's face was like; I can imagine he was smirking a big greasy New York City smirk. He looks at me more intently now and says, "Alright, I'll start you off at $16,000 and you can start today." Now, mind you, I've been out interviewing for the past three months with the big shops in the city, all that I could get into that is. Those shops were offering $17,000 to $20,000 for assistant account executives so I wasn't quite sure about an offer of $16,000. I sat up straight, looked Marty right in the eyes and said "Gee Marty, everyone else is offering $17,000 to $20,000... what do you say?" He looked at me more sternly this time and said, "All right, $17,000 not another penny. Get out of here."

I worked on some pretty exciting things for a 22-year-old. Kinney Shoes, the Cadillac dealer marketing Association of Atlanta, Dyanson art galleries and the occasional Footlocker ad as well. During this time, the industry was beginning to go through the initial consolidation stages. My agency, Sawden and Bess, had been acquired/merged with ACR and DHB; we were to be known as ACR/DHB & Bess. I stayed around for a few years after that merger and learned a lot. We moved our offices downtown to 16 E. 32nd St. where I occasionally roomed with a group of flight attendants, but that's another story altogether. I was really getting in the groove of being a New York City junior ad guy. It was around that time I got a call from an agency in Dallas that I thought was pretty cool. The Richards group called to see if I wanted to move to Dallas to be an account executive for a few of their accounts. I thought this sounded great and so I took the job. As it turns out my initial learning and perception of the ad business was from a strategically lead agency point of view, not a creative one. Upon arrival at the Richards group it was pretty clear that the creative side of the shop ran everything, which didn't sit too well for this young man who had just cut his teeth on Madison Avenue and had seen some of the best strategy in the business. I stayed only one year at Richards group. From there I went on to the promotion side of things; I figured I might as well learn that aspect of the industry as well. I had a great time working on Labatt's and Rolling Rock beer creating consumer promotions for on and off premise accounts. It was just the kind of work for a young, 20-something guy that gets you hooked on the industry. A few years later I got into the food and drink side of things on the business-to-business end at a full blown foodservice focused agency. As it turned out, I had taken a job with 3 ex-Missouri ad people who had relocated to Dallas to start their own shop, and to do it better than where they came from. I learned the foodservice business from some very smart people on some great accounts. Well, it came down to this, we were working on Tyson beef and pork while another agency in Missouri, in fact the same one these 3 founders had left, was working on Tyson chicken. Tyson put the account into review with the aim of consolidating all their proteins into one shop. We pitched, we lost the account and ultimately I was recruited by that Missouri agency to come run part of the beef and pork business they had just taken from the agency I was currently working for. Which, as it turns out was a pretty good idea because the other person they recruited was my new girlfriend. We decided to go to Missouri and make a go of it.

After settling into the Midwest lifestyle and five years at Noble and Associates, I grew bored with this foodservice gig and really wanted a taste of the beer business again. Zipatoni was the leading promotion shop in St. Louis at the time. I knew a person or two there and let them know I wanted to be back in the beer business. Before I knew it I had an offer to join as an Account Director at Zipatoni. By this time my then girlfriend from Texas was now my wife and we have a three-year-old son. After just three short years in St. Louis we returned to Noble and Associates. I would lead the retail promotion (early Shopper Marketing) and my wife would lead the foodservice division. It seemed as though this ad career thing was really beginning to work out and I was having a good time doing it. Five more years was all it took at Noble and Associates for me to realize I was growing bored once again. It was time to make another move and hopefully the last. I approached their competitor, who happened to be in the same market, with an offer to join on as their Business Development lead. As it turned out, they were in growth mode themselves and it was good timing.

My time at Marlin company, which ultimately became Marlin Network, was some of the most fulfilling of my career. I started as Business Development, grew into the position of Growth and Innovation and after an ESOP, settled into Innovation and M&A. We were doing such a good job growing and earning that we became attractive to one of the largest sales and marketing companies in the industry. In 2014 I received a call inquiring as to whether or not we would like to sell. Our Board of Directors decided it would be a good idea for the shareholders if we were to sell. In September 2015, Marlin Network was acquired by Advantage Solutions of Irvine, California and we became part of a very large multi-national solution provider inside their marketing division. While I had nothing against Advantage Solutions or being part of the big machine, I did have a certain special place in my heart for the entrepreneurial independent owners of the ad world. I decided at that time I would leave the organization and set up a consulting firm with the goal to help independent advertising/marketing agencies grow and/or exit. I would focus on new business, innovation, training, mergers and exit strategies, cultural growth and all around business development efforts.

Today, Austin Amplifies works with independent ad agencies of all sizes, all around the globe. And on this day, I decided it was time to write some of it down.

"Permission to win" is a phrase I've used for years. I use it when talking to individuals about their potential and how to get there. I use it as it relates to areas where an agency has the ability to enter into and win with new clients, and so much more. You see, "Permission to win" is the posture it takes to do the work required to win a new piece of business, enter into a new strategic adjacency or consider a new market penetration strategy. "Permission to win" is the attitude we must have to win in a competitive industry like advertising, promotion, PR, digital, experiential, et cetera. There's so much to consider when adopting a posture of "permission to win," that I decided this would be where I began to write and publish some thoughts.

In this book, <u>Permission To Win</u>, I'll share my approach to creating a culture of growth. The four areas I'll focus on include assessing the realities of your shop, preparing the tools you need to gain awareness and that "permission to win," the science of prospecting, and the art of pitching to win. We'll cover topics like understanding your USP and what the most leverageable equities of your proposition really are, leading to the strategic adjacencies where we have "permission to win." We'll explore understanding your talent and service offerings to the degree it's relevant to your existing core business and the strategic adjacencies we've identified. We'll cover the role that training occupies in the overall choreography of growth and why being involved in the industry of your clients is so important in solidifying your expertise. You'll learn how to identify the right conversation of your focused vertical and where you fit into that conversation. We'll explore what to do with that conversation insight and how to turn it into an inbound and outbound campaign strategy that draws prospects closer to you. We will take a look at the pitch process and the art of pitching to win. We'll lay down tips and approaches for competitive pitching that may very well be contrary to how you look at it today. And last, but certainly not least, let's get realistic about creating a plan; a plan that includes full transparency with your entire agency to foster accountability around that plan.

For now, preparation for reading this book includes being honest and objective about your business or team and the ability to create thought leadership around the growth of your business and where you have Permission to Win today.

Cheers,
DVA

Overview:
Assess, Prepare, Prospect, Pitch

Permission to win. What does it really mean anyway? Who are we seeking permission from? Do we really need permission? All of this begs the question *how* do we gain permission? The answers to all of these questions and so many more you're probably thinking right now, will be answered in the following chapters. Suffice to say, for now at least, that it all comes down to creating an environment where everyone feels safe enough to be completely vulnerable and share 100% of their gifts. We are, after all, in the creative thinking business and to be really good at what we do, we need everyone contributing at the highest level. What this all boils down to is creating an environment built on Trust and Respect. Now I could leave it there and call it done. However, what I've learned over the years is that it has taken a career of management and leadership experimentation to uncover what it takes to create a trusting and respectful environment. We are human after all, which means it's in our nature to be suspicious and, yes, even paranoid at times about our own abilities. We begin to question, judge and go through all the other ugly human emotions that poke their head up once we have had an opportunity to think it over more thoroughly. So, you see, while it's a simple credo, its academic unless you are "all in" on doing what it takes to create a culture of growth, one which will set you and your agency up for "permission to win."

The approach I use when working with agencies is quite simple and intuitive. In fact it's what you probably often prescribe to your agency clients. Assess, Prepare, Prospect, Pitch. These are the four areas we'll focus on.

So what can you expect? Unfortunately there really is no "silver bullet." Instead, it's a focused, deliberate effort to build an ever evolving business development approach. That approach begins with an objective assessment of exactly who you are and what you have to work with. Without this assessment you couldn't understand the tools you're missing or need to polish to be successful. Once we have the tools we need to be confident, we're in a position to actively prospect against a target we know we can bring value to. The pitch is where it all culminates and it is where the art of a trusting and respectful culture really shines through.

So what gives me "permission to win" in this conversation? I suppose it has to do with my love for the business, my enjoyment of working in the industry and my passion to see others succeed, not to mention the success I had in building agencies and agency networks for myself and others along the way. Coming up through account service into planning departments and ultimately the innovation space around food and drink for products and menu, I've been a part of and observed both competent and questionable agency environments. I've experienced firsthand the effects of a fear based culture, and the fruits of a trusting, respectful culture. While it's arguable that either can be effective in the short-term, the fact remains that long term sustainable growth can only survive in a trusting and respectful culture. And a "permission to win" attitude can only thrive in an agency that believes they have the expertise in a specific vertical that sets them far above their competition. That expertise can only take root when everyone in the agency trusts and respects the gifts and contributions of every other person in the agency. Everyone has value to offer and it's the leaderships job to make sure everyone is in the right place, and, as many of us know, that place can change for folks over time.

Consider for a moment if this sounds like your agency. We have creative folks who've decided that the account service folks and planners really don't understand the nuances of the customers/consumers that we're targeting on behalf of our clients. And as a result they have taken it upon themselves to act as the planner or account manager for that piece of business while at the same time producing and delivering on the creative. Now this may sound like you have a hero amongst you but what you really have here is a dastardly disruptor. In actuality this creative hero who, is taking on all of the duties of the planner and account services because he or she felt like they were not doing a good job, can't possibly be contributing 100% around the area that we expect them to be experts in, writing or art direction. Not to mention what it's doing to the disruption of a collaborative working environment from those who resent someone else trying to step in and do their job for them. Oh and by the way, who really wants to work at an agency as a planner or an account executive when you get over run by your creative partners? Not a healthy place to work, not a sustainable cultural vibe.

That scenario can go the other way as well. The planners have decided that they're better creative directors than the creative directors we have on staff and so they've decided that they'll write the headlines, layout design or direct the concept. Nothing good is going to come of that either. So let's focus on understanding what it means to trust and respect everyone's role at the agency. A trust and respect mindset would say "you should expect that I am doing everything in my power to progress my particular craft, the area that I contribute to the overall deliverable for a client, and I likewise am expecting you to do the same." If everyone focuses on doing their job to the best of their abilities, we shouldn't have an issue of trust or respect. We are creating a more symbiotic working environment, one which gives us "permission to win" because we're surrounded by experts in their fields rather than heroes trying to fix the world. The agency business is a bit like a Hero/Zero Roller Coaster ride (picture this for a moment.... One day you are a hero, the next a zero because it truly is all about your last idea, campaign, client win, etc... like a roller coaster you will go up and you will go down and then do it all over again). So, a little grace for those on the zero end of the ride at the moment will go a very long way in creating trust and respect. Remember, your ride is on the same track. In my experience, most issues and cultural rubs inside the agency among teams can generally be eradicated with a little time to let it pass, a bucket full of grace and, oh yes, a glass of wine seems to help.

Here are few thoughts to consider as you start to ease into the process.

- Approaching new business without a full business development strategy is only half the job.
- New business is not like client business.
- New business is about generating awareness and interest and selling yourself.
- People/clients still buy on emotional response. We are in the relationship business we've got to start there.
- You can't schedule new business pitches and certainly can't schedule wins.
- We must understand the business of our clients business if we're expected to be seen as experts by them.
- We don't have to take every invitation to participate in a pitch that comes along. Some of them aren't worth it, and others are not winnable.

- Create content that's timely and relevant and has a real perspective. People want to know you have an opinion.
- Take those opinions and insights and publish, speak, counsel, be quoted, and go on tour with it.
- Your website is your calling card. It's the first place a prospect goes before they ever call you. In fact, 100% of decisions to engage with an agency started with a website visit.
- Training is a proactive ingredient to success. Don't mail it in, innovate through it.
- Be involved in the industries of your clients.
- Understand the conversation of your clients' industry and form expert opinions about it.
- Engage in the conversation of your clients' industry and even lead it.

And remember this one very important thing: creative and strategic services are *bought* and not sold. Ultimately they are services, not products. It takes time for prospects to choose you. Which is why it's so important to be in the industries you profess to be experts in; and be there often.

Another aspect of creating your winning culture is the power of an independent mindset. Regardless if you are the sole owner, part of a group or report up through a network, an independent mindset can set you apart from the rest. If you have the latitude to make decisions that are right for you and yours, you can invoke the power of an independent mindset. Here are a handful of independent mindset characteristics you can consider how to leverage in your favor:

- Entrepreneurial by nature.
- Uncomplicated motivations (greater flexibility and objectivity).

- Willing to work to a common solution.
- Personal attention.
- Nimble and flexible.
- Willingness to pioneer.
- Ability to adjust to client and marketplace needs.
- Problem solver VS solution provider.

Leveraging your abilities and gifts of an independent mindset can be liberating as you compete in a sea of corporate minded agency competitors. Just imagine what you can accomplish if you adopt this simple perspective.

The Way I See it

The way I have always approached business development can be likened to how we approached helping our clients grow. I spent most of my career agency life in the Consumer Packaged Goods world, both Business to Consumer (B2C) and Business to Business (B2B). Regardless of the channel, it was our job to help the brands we represented grow in a competitive, and often times commoditized, environment. Business development is fundamentally and intellectually the same approach. That approach goes something like this:

1. Start with an objective assessment of who we are today.
2. Define the opportunities we can win in today.
3. Explore multiple growth strategies to create viable platforms for real growth.
4. Work hard to create true value. (Because value is where the margin is... service alone is a commodity.)
5. Identify those we have "permission to win" with.
6. Understand the "conversation" of their channel/category.
7. Invest in knowing the business of their business.

8. Position ourselves as experts in their category.
9. Make sure our target knows we exist and what we offer.
10. Train our teams up to be an extension of our expertise.
11. Engage in the industry of our clients in an objective and thought provoking way.
12. Commit to continuous learning and innovation in the crafts of our business and our clients.

And when it comes down to a competitive pitch scenario, make sure our passion and expertise shine.

CHAPTER 1

ASSESSMENT

Objectivity:

Beginning to create a culture of growth which will provide you with "permission to win," starts with an objective assessment of your agency. What kind of agency would you identify as? Creative led, strategy led, client led, industry led, etc.... there are so many ways to view yourself. Regardless of how you identify, it really does not matter unless your industry clients agree and see you as a valuable partner to them. Funny how that works, isn't it?

If you are not sure what kind of agency you are, ask yourself how your competitors view you and what kind of reputation you have among your markets and client base. It's a humbling exercise to be sure and one which, if you are honest with your opinion of yourself, will provide the canvas for your evolution. Beyond how you "feel" there are the facts and realities of who you are and what you do. Assessing your agency strengths and weaknesses informs how and where you can intentionally adjust for the future and create a winning culture of growth. Beginning with a full assessment and understanding of your current state of business includes , but is not limited to:

- The economics of your business
- Understanding your core expertise
- Your declared focused vertical

- The realities of your focused verticals' economic outlook
- Your handle on the issues and conversation of your focused vertical
- Competitive agency set inside this focused vertical
- Viable strategic adjacencies for growth and new client acquisition
- Current talent and service audit/gap analysis
- Current capabilities narrative/presentation
- Your value proposition
- Your Unique Selling Proposition (USP)
- Growth goals
- Courage to commit to growth goals (accountability to your agency)
- Training regiment
- Content creation process
- PR/Marketing/Awareness
- Outbound new business efforts
- Prospecting: strategy/approach/qualifying
- Industry trade involvement
- Current client retention strategy (staffing, initiatives, cross training)
- Industry reputation
- Current RFI response style
- Current RFP response style
- Current pitch strategy and approach
- Your ability to onboard clients well
- Your ability to absorb new talent into your culture
- The health of your culture
- Ability to identify your culture culprits
- Your appetite for innovation and continued learning
- Your appetite for change

Beyond all the functional aspects of understanding your business and truly being objective about the assessment, you really must be honest with yourself about your desire to work at this growth. And what I mean by that is are you having fun, is this fulfilling, do you want to do it again next year, are you making the kind of living you want to make, are you looking for a way out, are you looking for a motivation to continue? There are so many things we really must consider during this objective assessment of our business before we can truly move forward with creating this culture of growth that will give us "permission to win."

Economics

Let's start with understanding the economics of your business. Do you know where you make money, do you know which clients are profitable, do you know which employees are the most productive? So often I ask agency owners which are their best client? Meaning, which are the most profitable? Often times they can't answer. Well, it's really hard to know where you're going and where you have "permission to win" if you don't understand where you are winning currently. We've all heard the saying, "a profitable business will hide a lot of sins." While this is true it also leaves us completely vulnerable on a less than profitable year. Which is why getting a handle on your P&L is so critical to setting you up for success. Since most agencies still subscribe to timesheet tracking, understanding the profitability of an account is not that difficult.

Sometimes we deliberately don't do the analysis because we don't want to know we are losing money. If this is you (be honest), then you have a very big decision to make before you go any further. Do you want to continue to operate the way you have, OR, are you ready to really dive in and understand the state of your business to the degree that your decisions are driven more by fact than emotion? It's a fundamental shift and one that is liberating once you make the decision to act on it. Do yourself a favor, and get an understanding of the profitability of your business, account by account, and industry by industry, if you have more than one focus. You'll need this insight when we get to the talent and service audit exercises. If finances are not your strong suit, then hire a creative minded controller or CFO if you can keep them busy. The business insights from a financial perspective are liberating. If you simply go with your "gut" on how well you are doing, you may find yourself with a stomachache the first time you get into a real margin/revenue squeeze. It's always better to KNOW than FEEL when it comes to numbers and your finances. Hire a strong financial leader and be clear what success looks like to you, not to them. Remember it's your company, not theirs, so you define success.

Expertise

The next thing we really need to understand as you assess your business, is where your expertise lies. I like to make a distinction here between experience and expertise. If you currently are not focused on one or two or even three specific business verticals, then you may believe your expertise lies in the functionality of your service offering. I highly recommend to those who hang their expertise on functionality/services, to declare a business vertical to focus on to become experts in. Because competition among service providers far exceeds competition among industry/vertical experts, It's really that simple. If however, your functional expertise far exceeds those around you, or in your market, then perhaps that is your main focus.

The distinction between experience and expertise really has most to do with your ability to understand and add value to the business of your clients business. When your clients see you as a valuable resource and asset to achieving their goals, you've reached expert status. If, however, you prefer to concede to someone else on the bigger business building discussions, and remain focused on the execution of others ideas, I would suggest you are experienced yet not an expert in that particular vertical. The good news is, if you desire to level up from experience to expert level status, you can get there with a focused and deliberate plan and steady effort.

One of my favorite agency engagements included working with an individual who truly understood the value of being intentional. "The intentionality," he would say, "Is missing in my rigger and I don't know how to bring it back." In this particular case it was really less about bringing something back as it was about being deliberate about resurrecting something that had been there all along, which is to say, the passion for the business. The passion for the business had always been there, yet the intentionality to learn new things and remain relevant had slipped a bit. Once we dusted that off and brought it into the light, the trajectory of growth for this particular agency was nothing short of spectacular. By calling into being, the need for a growth vision session, with his leadership team, we were able to collaboratively assess, prepare, prospect and pitch to win. I'm happy to report that three years after our initial session this particular agency has been growing by leaps and bounds in the focused vertical areas we identified during the vision sessions. The "intentionality" we put behind the effort coupled with that objective assessment of who they were and where they wanted to go was really all it took. Identifying the talent and service gaps relative to their competitive set in the verticals they wanted to focus in, was a very insightful exercise and one that I encourage everyone to do. It's the beginning of understanding your value proposition in a way that can create a unique selling proposition to your highly targeted prospects. The bonus of this exercise is that you now have a roadmap for not only hiring and acquiring, but also training and content development. You begin to build confidence in identifying the conversations of your industries and focused verticals and engage in them in a way that you've never experienced before. Why? Because you're now armed with experts that you personally trained up or added to your staff that continue to push forward your insight through expertise. This is a very liberating point in the pivot or evolution of an agency. A point which you will look back on, and realize that what it took to get where you are today is a deliberate, focused, intentional effort that all began with a truly objective assessment of who you are and an understanding of where you want to be. Not all that dissimilar than what we do for our clients on a daily basis.

Where do you want to be? What does the future look like even three or five years out? Have you considered the amount you would like to earn, have you considered the number of core clients you'd like to have, have you thought about the number of people you'd like to have employed? When I work closely with agencies on their assessment, I focus on three areas to kick off the conversation of this growth vision session. Those three areas are: revenue, people and the number of core clients. You see, it's the simplest way to sort a breakdown when considering where one wants to grow. Let's start with the current year. For example purposes we will make a few assumptions about this fictitious agency. Let's assume Agency XYZ. No that's a crummy name, we can think of something better than that.

How about the Contemplative Creative Agency? Yeah, that's better. The Contemplative Creative Agency has 21 people today and they have six clients. Of the six clients, two of them make up 75% of their $3 million revenue. If we asked the owner what their USP, unique selling proposition, is, she would say that they are in the business of consumer/shopper marketing inside the CPG channel. Specifically her client base today, those two large ones that make up 75% of her business, are a frozen pizza manufacturer and an ice cream brand. So, while the Contemplative Creative Agency may very well be in the business of leveraging consumer and shopper insights, I'm suggesting that they're really in the business of understanding snacking and dessert consumption habits of frozen food consumers which has a much deeper value proposition attached to it than the functional aspects of leveraging shopper marketing best practices. If we fully understand the habits, of the specific target, we are in a better position to lead them to the point of purchase by leveraging the entire retail purchase journey. This is an example of taking our expected functional selling proposition, and expanding it further through delineation to create a more ownable unique selling proposition.

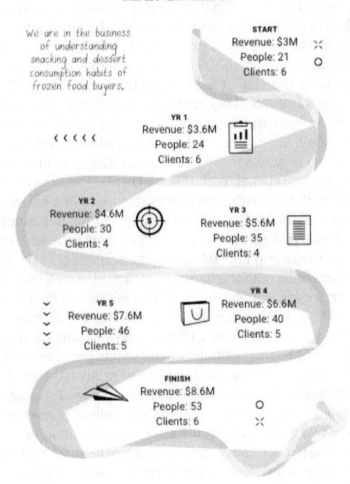

Contemplative Creative Agency

SAMPLE 5 YEAR TRAJECTORY

We are in the business of understanding snacking and dessert consumption habits of frozen food buyers.

START
Revenue: $3M
People: 21
Clients: 6

YR 1
Revenue: $3.6M
People: 24
Clients: 6

YR 2
Revenue: $4.6M
People: 30
Clients: 4

YR 3
Revenue: $5.6M
People: 35
Clients: 4

YR 5
Revenue: $7.6M
People: 46
Clients: 5

YR 4
Revenue: $6.6M
People: 40
Clients: 5

FINISH
Revenue: $8.6M
People: 53
Clients: 6

Now that we have our baseline, it's time to consider what growth looks like over the next five years. Considering the realities of growth relative to office space, overhead, payroll, insurance, taxes etc., It's something we really must pay attention to and be realistic about how much growth we have the appetite for. A simple breakdown on the growth trajectory based on where we want to be in the next five years (and for this example let's assume that means doubling), begins with stepping it out over the three years in between. The Contemplative Creative Agency decided that if they're really honest with themselves, being a $6 million shop in five years was a pretty good goal. In keeping with the rule of thumb of full-time equivalents to AGI ratio, (which, by the way, it is 7FTE's/$1million), that will put them at 42 people. They also agreed that having the same amount of clients they have today (six) would be great, they would like the revenue to be spread out a little more evenly so they're not as vulnerable as they are today with their top two clients. With this goal in mind and the desire to bring those existing six clients into more of a balanced alignment, the leading growth strategy for the Contemplative Creative Agency is in growing existing business with an eye to margin/EBITDA. While the academics of sketching something out for a five year growth plan look good on paper, we are acutely aware of the realities of client management and what can actually happen over a five-year period with those clients. Thus, simply focusing on growing existing business would be a bit shortsighted and risky. I would suggest to the Contemplative Creative Agency that what they really need to do is have dual growth strategies outlined which leverage their unique selling proposition. These two growth strategies will focus on leveraging core expertise (frozen consumption habits in the snack and dessert categories) and identifying strategic adjacencies where they have a natural positioning and "permission to win" with their current USP.

The realities of your focused verticals' economic outlook
Your handle on the issues
and conversation of your focused vertical

Once you are comfortable with your decision to focus in certain business verticals, we must consider the growth potential inside that vertical and be ready to focus even further in to maximize the growth space of that vertical. For example, in the case of the Contemplative Creative Agency and their focus on frozen snacks and desserts, we know that pizza and ice cream are both under scrutiny from a health perspective and yet, both are strong categories in the frozen aisle. If we are going to focus our efforts in this category, what are the best chances for innovative growth? Consider the driving trends here, the new brands and products entering the space and how the shelf set is shifting. Understanding the future of the frozen aisle and in particular the implications to ice cream and pizza, is certainly something the frozen retail buyers will want to be introduced to. This is a good example of contributing to the conversation of the industry we choose to focus on. Operating in a commoditized category, such as frozen food, is not without opportunity, we just have to be diligent in looking in the right places and creating opportunity from insight. Stay sharp, look deep it's there.

Regarding the conversation of the industries we focus on, there are many ways to engage, and a multitude of narratives to consider as we stoke it. Everything from the syllabus and agendas of the trade associations and conferences, to the headlines from the industry trade publications. Consider the last trade show you attended. Thinking back on your time as you walked the floor, recall taking into account the banner headers in the many booths. Could you put a headline to that experience? It's almost a game with me. I like to turn a three day walking event at a tradeshow into a simple headline. For example, a recent food ingredient trade show that I attended, was summed up like this: "Pea protein and coconut everything." Now I'll admit that while it's somewhat comical, it really helps to make the point and drive all the observations to a macro level. So, considering the last trade event of the verticals you focus on, how would you headline that event experience?

The headlines we take away from trade events and the topics of the curriculum in speakers and panels, are the narrative of the industry we're focused on. If we take all that into consideration, and add to it observations beyond the immediate channel, we begin to form our perspectives and opinions about that industry. Many of these conversation topics are polarizing or even argumentative inside the industry itself. Rather than feel like you're forced to choose a side, have an opinion about how you can help clients navigate that conversation and debate inside their industry. The objectivity of your third-party perspective on a polarizing industry topic can be just the type of value potential clients need to choose you. Because right or wrong, within the conversation it is real, and the reality of the existence inside the industry today has a lot to do with how you navigate through it. So be seen as the navigator, create a narrative for their brands inside the industry in a way that helps them rise above the debate, and take a strong stance one way or another. But remember, you don't have to choose a side, you just have to be objective about navigating.

Being part of the conversation is mandatory, leading the conversation is the goal. First, to be considered experts in any part of the industries we focus on, we have to be students of the conversation. What I mean by that is we have to be open to, and willing to engage in, two-way conversations in the industry. We can do this in many ways like, publishing, speaking, sitting on panels, judging, etc. The point is, do it. The other thing about engaging in the conversation that is very important, is to remember to bring others along for the ride. If only one or two inside the agency have a handle on the conversation and the narrative of that conversation as it relates to brands, we're not doing what we should in terms of training. Bring others along, get them exposed to the conversation, engage them in the debate internally, and help them form their own opinion.

An engaging way to bring the conversation to the agency for everyone to engage in, is good ole fashioned "lunch and learns." Think of it like this: pick a topic, share that among your staff, encourage everyone to read up on this subject, and show up for a spirited conversation about it during lunch one day. The simple act of verbalizing an opinion or comment about a topic is the type of confidence instilling behavior we need to demonstrate inside our agencies to create experts. While white papers and perspective papers are a fantastic way to summarize our opinions, nothing can beat the act of on your feet live, conversations about the topic. Remember, we're training up experts in our ranks, and we must be able to test their mettle on the debate/discussion about that topic.

Understanding the conversation of your industry, and the ability to create a narrative around it for your clients, is not only important to maintain relevance with existing clients but also the fodder for your content creation. Once we have this narrative lined out, the ability to turn that into content, in so many ways, is really endless. This becomes the guiding rudder for your content outline around prospecting. It is important to know that there is a cadence to the conversation in any industry and it usually aligns with the main industry event topics for that vertical.

Competitive agency set inside this focused vertical

Viable strategic adjacencies for growth and new client acquisition

Your competitive set might not look like you think. Once you've chosen to focus on a particular business vertical, your competitive set looks a little less like other agencies, and more like in-house and consulting firms. A strong consulting firm working inside your chosen vertical, is 1 to 2 key hires away from competing with you as an agency.

While some statistics will suggest there are over 120,000 agencies in the U.S. today, there are upwards of 35-40,000 advertising and PR agencies alone, *even* if we broke that down by specialization of agencies, meaning full-service, SEO, digital, PR and media. Now, not to be a defeatist, but the thought of having thousands of competitors is daunting. Consider now the amount of competitors you have in a focused vertical. It's probably more in the dozens. This is the competitive set I can get okay with. However, we are now faced with competing against in – house, overseas, or contract labor. As we start to consider our competitive set, let's be realistic about who we're actually competing with, and make sure our USP has real value.

Our unique selling proposition is something we should really spend time determining. For it's that USP that will launch us into strategic adjacencies where we have "permission to win." Determining which strategic adjacencies actually make sense for us to explore, has as much to do with our core expertise as it does the leverageable aspects of our selling proposition. If we deconstruct the value of our selling proposition to determine which portion of it is leverageable, we can then build the bridge to the winning strategic adjacencies. For example, if our USP is that we are in the business of helping hotel franchisors attract franchisees, then we have permission to explore other service model industries which franchise. Being experts in the hotel vertical is not the leveragable value here, it's the franchisor/franchisee relationship insights which provides the bridge to adjacent verticals such as restaurants and muffler shops.

Current talent and service audit/gap analysis

Having a good handle on what we offer our clients, and what they value, is a great place to start an assessment of our talent and service offering. Anyone who's ever been responsible for maintaining a client, can relate to this need to carry around in their head at all times the make-up of their talent and services against the client. It looks like a simple matrix. Across the top we have our clients, and down the side we have the services we offer.

Service Audit

WE PROVIDE		RETAIL/LSM	RESTAURANT	B2B
Strategic Planning/Concepting	−$	×	×	×
Media Planning/Buying	−$	×/o	×	
Marketing Plan Development	−$		o	
Web Design	$			o
Branding	$$$	×	×	×
Direct Marketing	$	o	o	o
Print Production	$$	×	×	
Digital Production	$$	×	×	
Project Management	$	×	×	×
Video/Photography	$$	×	×	×
E-Mail Marketing/Direct	$	×/o	×/o	o
Account Planning	−$	o	o	
Menu Boards	$	×	×	
Lead Generation/Nurture	$	o	o	o
Digital/Social	−$	o	o	o
Packaging	$	×	×	

COMPETITORS PROVIDE	RETAIL/LSM	RESTAURANT	B2B
Influencer Marketing	×	×	×
SEO / SEM	×/o	×	
Content Creation	o	o	o
PR			o
Industry Trade Shows	×	×	×
Market Research	o	o	o

× Currently Offer   O Opportunity   ×/O Currently Offer $ Profitability

As we go service by service and client by client, we can check the box or not. When we put this exercise on paper, however, it reveals to us the opportunity gaps we have with current clients using existing services. While that's informative and can certainly help us understand where we're leaving opportunity on the table so to speak, it's not the whole story. Consider for a moment adding another section to your matrix. Add below all of your existing services that you offer your clients today, all the services you know your clients buy from other vendors. Great, now you've identified where you're missing. The good news about this exercise is that it now informs a few things. Not only have you identified your service gap, you've also informed your training curriculum and hiring needs. You see, we have two ways to go with this. Number one, you can concede the services you don't offer that others do, or, number two, you can make a plan to close the gap and get the services onboard at the agency and for your clients.

One last exercise with this existing matrix includes the analysis of where we make money. Go back to the portion of the matrix that includes all the services you offer and rank them by profitability. This is also quite revealing. If you have a lot of services that you offer current clients that you don't make any money on, you should stop. Now I know that sounds like common sense but you'd be surprised how many agencies I work with that don't, or they rationalize the need to take a loss on a particular service to keep the account.

This exercise has proven to be one of the most valuable of all those that I take my agency clients through. And while it's virtually in our head all the time, I encourage everyone to put it to paper.

Value Proposition

What do you offer that is truly valuable to the clients and industry you serve? The million dollar question (literally, often times). If you have never taken the time to identify your value proposition to you clients, today is the day. The distinctions between your value proposition and your unique selling proposition (USP) are subtle. Think about what your clients might say about the value you provide to their business, this is your value proposition. Defined as:

val·ue prop·o·si·tion
noun

1. (in marketing) an innovation, service, or feature intended to make a company or product attractive to customers.

Your value proposition is where your margin lies. Innovation is a key part of this definition. Innovative thinking, process, approach, execution, economics, etc. The innovation can come in many varieties. Be sure you are staying relevant with your value proposition. Remember, innovation is perishable. Today's innovation is tomorrow's commodity.

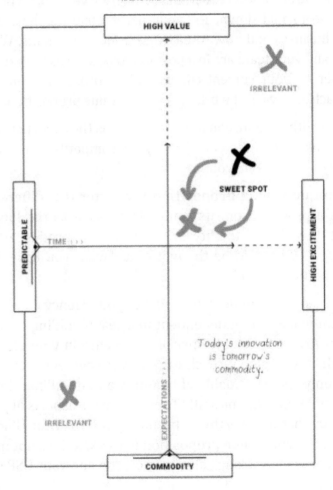

Increased time and expectations shape the path to commoditization for all innovation. It truly is just a matter of time before today's innovation has become an expected part of our lives and/or business. You think I'm kidding? Ponder the first iPod or iPhone capability. It was outlandishly innovative when it rolled out. Today, gen1 iPhone is...... you get it.

Once you become an expert in your chosen vertical, it's pretty simple to nail down; its' your perspective on the industry/business and how to navigate it for your clients. When you and your team are in a position to be seen as the experts either by your current clients and/or prospects, your approach and ways of working are your value proposition.

On the other hand, consider your USP as the aspect of your offering that raises you above your competition in a way that is ownable by you.

A **unique selling proposition** is a factor that differentiates a product from its competitors, such as the lowest cost, the highest quality or the first-ever product of its kind. A **USP** could be thought of as "what you have that competitors don't."

Consider for a moment what makes your agency unique. Is it that you are an independent in a sea of holding companies? Are you the only specialized agency in your chosen vertical with global reach or Midwest coverage? Are you the only agency capable of handling a multimillion dollar account with existing staff? There are many aspects of your agency that are worthy of becoming part of your USP. If, however, your value proposition is weak, it does not matter. Focus on a strong value proposition and your USP will follow.

Courage to commit to growth goals (accountability to your agency)

Once we have our growth strategy and platforms identified, and we have laid out our 90 day action plan to accomplish it, it's time to openly and honestly commit to the rest of your team/agency the plans. Nothing says accountability like a companywide meeting to unveil the plan, the approach and the desired outcomes. Declaring you will do what is necessary to proactively grow the agency is a liberating feeling, and it's fulfilling to know you will be held accountable. I recommend announcing the intentions of the plan right away and follow up with a formal plan within 30 days. Regardless if the agency is 13 or 1,300 people, you'll want to formalize your plan with the rest of the team members to ensure it is clear where you are headed. Don't make the mistake/assumption that everyone is clear on the plans, the reality is even those who may have participated in some way may not be clear on the full picture. Declare it like it's a revolution and then ask them to hold you accountable. They will thank you later and even if they don't, you'll see it in their actions. We are in the communications business and yet we often pass on the opportunity to communicate within our own walls. Don't let the opportunity to lead your team pass you by because you don't believe they want to know the details. They do and they want to know you are committed.

Training Regiment

Training is often overlooked and/or considered the job of someone else. The reality is that when we are in a growth posture (and btw, we are always in a growth posture or we will be in a die posture), it's important to make sure the team is equipped and ready to take the vision forward with confidence. We've likely all had first-hand experience, or know of an agency where their "lack of bench strength" was the beginning of the end for them. You see, even if every other aspect of the business development approach is addressed and addressed well, if we fall short on training up our team, we'll be in a situation where we bottleneck the work for clients because not enough people have the skills and confidence to move the client forward. This is a situation that can be avoided. For now, know that training is something which must be addressed in the assessment phase to identify just how far you'll need to go/grow in this area to be competitive and positioned to win. Consider not only the functional training you are providing, but more importantly, the expertise training in the verticals you have declared your focus.

Content Creation Process

The ability to create content for your clients is a key indicator of your ability to create your own. At this point in communications history if you are not creating content for your clients you are likely not a full service shop and thus, may need some help addressing this need. If, however, you are indeed creating content for your clients, you need to be doing the same for yourself. There is a lot interwoven into the content discussion and we will explore this much deeper when we dive into the prospect section of the book. For now, suffice to say, this skill set is needed inside your shop whether you provide it as a paid service for your clients today or not.

PR/Marketing/Awareness/Outbound

"The cobblers kids have no shoes," we've all heard that one before, and it's true. When it comes to PR and marketing communications for our clients we're great at that. However, when it comes to marketing for ourselves, we tend to put it off or de-prioritize it because we're too busy. The reality is we likely know what to do, we just don't do it. Be honest with yourself about how much time you really put into focusing on your own marketing, and then ask yourself is it really all you can do.

Here's another saying we've all heard before "everything communicates, everything." If we don't feel like we need to be marketing ourselves because we get plenty of phone calls and invitations to participate in RFI's, think about how many we would have and the caliber of those invitations if we were proactive about our marketing. A big part of the assessment phase during this business development approach has as much to do with being real about what we have and don't have, as it is about what we need to have.

Besides what we're doing in terms of PR and marketing awareness, what specifically are we doing for our outbound effort? What are we doing to generate awareness among the targets we have identified? Think of it this way, when we received a phone call from someone who wants to work with us, how do we react? There are a few of ways we could react to this: A) We're excited that somebody thought enough of us that they called us and wanted us to work with them. Or, B) We take the call and realize halfway through they really have no budget and we wish they hadn't ever called to begin with. Or, C) We are excited that we got the call, we realize they don't have any money, but we say yes anyway because we're just not all that busy and "why not?" It could be fun. There is so much to unpack about this and we will in the preparation section of the book. For now, recognize what you are putting out there in terms of your PR/marketing/outbound awareness efforts and prepare to be ready to add to that effort, whatever it is, today.

Prospecting: Strategy/Approach/Qualifying

We turn the assessment lens now to our prospecting efforts. Again, this is an area where you will be best served if you are honest with yourself about the effort you are putting into proactive prospecting, not what you wish you had time to do.

Before we take a look at your current prospecting efforts, this feels like an appropriate spot to share what I have found to be true with so many of the agency owners I've "almost" worked with. I say almost because I often get calls from agency principals when they <u>need</u> revenue to fill a client or budget loss gap and they are in a panic. (by the way; that is *not* the time to seek the help.) The calls I receive from folks in this panic mode tend to have a tone of resentment, which I finally came to understand the cause of once I realized these folks called me as a last resort and somehow took the need to call as a sign of defeat on their part. Not a cool way to be receiving a call, yet it happens a couple of times a year at least. The conversation usually goes something like this:

Agency X Owner: Hi, Doug, I wanted to talk to you about new business.

DVA: Hi, X. Sure thing, happy to chat about business development with you. What is your current situation? *(by the way, "new business" is how many refer to what I ultimately help them see the difference in between business development and new business.)*

Agency X Owner: Our client's budgets are shrinking and we are not winning new clients so I need someone to go out there and bring in a few new clients for us.

DVA: I see, how have you been gaining new clients thus far?

Agency X Owner: Well, that's just it. We've had the clients we have now for quite some time and a few new ones have come in over the past couple of years from past clients that left their brand and went to another, so we were fortunate enough to never have to "do new business."

DVA: Well, that's certainly a fine place to be. So why do you need help gaining new clients now?

Agency X Owner: Well, for some reason, our current client's budgets keep getting reduced and we are not able to keep the same revenue levels we once did. So, I need a sales person to go get us some new clients.

DVA: I see. Well I'm happy to chat but I must tell you that a sales person to go get you new clients might not be the solution. If you are open to a discussion about what it takes to create a business development approach, which will feed your agency with opportunity for the future, I'm happy to engage and share the approach I have honed in on over the years as an agency owner responsible for growth and innovation. My approach is a bit more involved than helping agency owners such as yourself go get new clients. While that is the end result, there is far more involved with the approach to get there than initially seems. I stand by this approach because I've used it myself to grow the network of agencies I was responsible for as well as helped many other independent agencies grow beyond where they thought possible. It's a full business development approach which includes new business, yet does not begin there.

Agency X Owner: Thanks. No offense, but I know what to do, I'm just too busy to do it so I need to hire a sales person to go out and get us new clients.

DVA: I see. Well, again, I'm not sure that's your solution but if you'd like to chat further I would suggest we set a time to discuss your business a bit deeper including, the economics, your staff, your services, your competition, your training regiment, your areas of influence and expertise, the categories you work in today and your involvement in those sectors, etc.

Agency X Owner: Yeah, no, I don't have time for that, I need new clients now so if you're interested let me know, if not, no worries, I'll keep looking.

DVA: Well, I'm not sure I'm the best fit for you then. You see, it will be difficult for me to help you market yourself unless I better understand who you are, where you've been, how prepared you are to compete in the arena you wish to compete in and whom you'll be up against. So, I'm going to have to pass on this opportunity and I wish you well. A few parting thoughts I'll leave you with to ponder though:

- Be suspect of anyone who says yes to your invitation. They may get you into a call or meeting, however, it may be the wrong kind of client for you. Perpetuation of the commoditization of our industry is rampant and there are certain short sighted decisions to do work for less than market value that have created this situation. Don't get caught in the trap.
- If it were that easy to "go get new clients" no one would need what I do.
- Until you have objectively assessed your business and prepare for a proactive awareness effort, you

will be in reactive new business mode. Unfortunately this mode is not sustainable and often not short term profitable.

- Regarding your shrinking client budgets: Are you sure they are shrinking or are they being diverted to partners who offer a more relevant set of services?
- We are in the service business and services are bought, not sold. As a result, a sales person may not be what you need, but rather a marketer may be more helpful.

Now, that was fun, and illustrative to be sure, however the sentiment is true. Often we find ourselves in denial about what we truly need to focus on to get the results we want. It's human nature, yes, but it's also something that, when we are conscious about it, can be overcome. So, I would suggest that as you are assessing your prospecting efforts, you shoot straight with yourself and, by extension, your agency, and allow yourself to be brutally honest. The specifics you'll want to look at include:

- Do you have a prospecting strategy? Or are you in reaction mode to incoming inquiries?
- If you do have a prospecting strategy, do you follow it? What are you doing today?
- Do you have a process in place to ensure you are identifying the "right" prospects?
- Are you qualifying your prospects to be sure they are the type of client you have "permission to win" with AND want to work with?
- Once you have identified the right prospects for you, are you proactively creating awareness among them?
- Are you constantly expanding and qualifying your prospecting pool?

There are so many ways we can begin to pivot out of a reactionary prospecting posture and we'll dive into those in the chapter that focuses on prospecting. For now, take note of what you are actually doing, not what you know you should be doing.

Industry Trade Involvement

"Understanding the business of your *client's* business." I keep emphasizing this point, but what does it mean? We must be as involved and committed to understanding how our clients make money, what their business model consists of, what their KPI's are, and who their competitors are, etc, as we are to communicating and promoting their products and services. One way we can contribute to that knowledge is by being involved in the events, trade shows, summits, conventions and association meetings happening in their particular industry. I like to joke that there is an association for everything. and go on to say. To prove my point I often refer to the Association Of Shitake Mushroom Growers of Southwest Missouri and while this is fictitious, there is indeed an American Mushroom Institute. You get my point there is an association or group to support just about any business you can imagine, so be aware of all those that support the work your clients do and get involved. We'll talk more about how to get the most out of industry involvement in the prospecting section. For now, if you are not aware of the events and forums supporting the business of your clients, dig in and find out.

Current Client Retention Strategy

There is a lot to consider about our current clients, not the least of which is how to retain and grow with them. However, before we can consider how we grow with them, we must first ensure we are retaining them. One of the quickest ways to go out of business is to have your current client portfolio erode. Duh, right? Super Captain Obvious, however, if you look at the attention we place on staying relevant and valued in the eyes of our current clients you'd agree it's something we need to be more deliberate about. While we can all agree it's a full time job simply servicing the current needs of our clients, it's just simply not enough if we want to keep and grow with them, we must also be leading them with creative thinking about their business as well as bringing them initiatives. This is another area where we know what we should be doing, however, rarely create the time to do it. It's in the same camp as "post mortems" on jobs to better understand how we can do it better the next time. Almost every agency I've been at talks about this and never does it. It's one of those check boxes on the brief or project file/folder that simply gets ignored because, we are too busy on the next project. Perhaps we are too busy on the next project because we continue to fail to learn from our past mistakes and round and round it goes.......frustrating indeed.

So don't let deliberate thought around client retention fall into the post mortem meeting category. Get real about what you are doing to not only keep your current clients satisfied and seeing value in what you do, but what you will be doing next to keep and grow with them. A few areas to consider in this assessment phase include:

- Services Offered: Are we industry ready with our service offerings? Or are we like the gal with a hammer and so every problem looks like a nail?
- Team Talent: Are you keeping your staff knowledgeable about the business of your client's business? If you are not, they cannot have the

creative problem solving skills they need to lead their client through the growth.

- **Cross Training Your Team:** Be sure your bench strength on any client goes deeper than you believe it needs to. If you are one team member departure away from having a client become vulnerable, you should probably mitigate that risk by introducing more team members. This also creates a healthy competition and relief to boredom which we'll dive into more in the preparation section.
- **Proactive Initiatives:** One of the top reasons given why clients leave their current agency is because they are not getting any new thinking from them. They have become order takers. There is a lot wrapped up in this one particular proactive approach. Not the least of which, is if your client "believes" they bring you all the ideas and you are simply executing them, they will grow frustrated by your invoices and lose confidence in your ability. This is bad.

Maintaining current clients and growing with them is the #1 Growth Platform we will explore as part of our overall business development planning section. Stay tuned. For now, be real about your current situation and be prepared to explore additional perspectives and approaches.

Industry Reputation

This next exploration about who you are is often a bit awkward for owners to discuss. When I ask what their reputation is in the industry/market, they sometimes pause as if they have never considered it. Well, the reality is, all your competitors, clients and possibly potential clients have a perception of who you are, regardless if it's right. So, I ask what their reputation is. Most commonly provide their positioning and or value proposition as their reputation, however that may not be accurate. I recall working at one particular agency who would tell you that their reputation was that they were the most creative agency in the southwest, which was arguable and probably true at the time however what they were known for was not that. Their reputation, what they were known for at the time, was their ability to chew up talent and grind their people to unimaginable lengths all for the sake of the client work. Now, if you are a client, you can pretend that the people were not being abused and, frankly, this was the late 80's and no one cared, but you could not deny that you liked that about them. If you were a potential client, you wanted some of that agency attention and if you were an associate, or wanted to be an associate, you were willing to put up with the abuse for a time to gain the resume builder that it was. So, you see, even when your reputation is not what you wish it were, it's still effective. Today we live in different times, thank goodness, and that type of perception/reputation would be damaging for all and luckily that particular agency no longer has the reputation as the "grinder." That said, it is important to understand what your reputation is in the world you operate in because to be believable and to position yourself to win, we must know the battle we have in front of us. So, be brutally honest about your reputation and if you really do not know what others think of you, just ask; I'm sure your competitors would love to tell you what they think of you. ☺

RFI/RFP/Pitch

Ahh, the cadence of what should be big opportunities for an agency. The formality of the RFI, RFP and the height of agency life, THE COMPETITIVE PITCH. There is so much to talk about here, and frankly this is where I truly loved to spend my time at the agency. Anyone who ever worked with me knows I lived for the opportunity to move through a formal process and took great pride in winning each step along the way. The pitch is something many never get to experience and is an area I spent most of my time in for the last 10 years of my formal agency career. There is nothing like it, and that's the truth. As you think about your approach to responding to formal client agency calls for project work and AOR, consider the many levels and forms proposals take and think about how you typically respond. Again, not how you know you should, but how you actually do. Each step in the RFI/RFP/Pitch process has a specific objective and yet, we sometimes forget that. The RFI is meant to winnow down the field of potential agencies. The RFP is meant to winnow down the field of qualified agencies and the pitch is meant to identify the best working partner for the clients. Any agency that makes it to the competitive pitch should consider this:

- Each agency in the pitch has the qualifications to do the work
- They have a champion on their side who voted them to the next round
- The others participating in the pitch have a champion on their side as well
- The work alone will not win the pitch
- The deck will not win the pitch, they are buying people, not a presentation
- Strategy alone will not win the pitch

- The pitch is not a meeting, it's a performance
- The pitch is not a training ground for your team
- Not everyone who participated in the prep of the pitch goes
- The cadence of the conversation during the pitch should reflect what it will be like to work with you

We'll dive deep into the entire RFI/RFP/Pitch approach later. For now, be real about the effort you put into responding to these formal types of requests.

Onboarding Clients Well and Including New Talent

Sometimes we wish for the BIG new opportunity or client and when it shows up we kind of lose our minds. You know what I mean. I'll never forget the time we won a new client worth a predicted $4mm in revenue and my CFO partner did not think we could handle it. The reality is he had no idea how to handle it because he was accustomed to managing, not creating, the revenue we produced and so, it was a scary thought for him, especially because this one particular client win represented more revenue than one entire agency in the group at the time. I get it, and it's scary but not overwhelming. The CEO and I had no reservations about handling it and everyone rallied. That client is still with that agency today, go figure. Now that is not the way it always goes. We've all heard about the agency that won the big client and choked on it. It is my belief they choked on it because they did not give themselves permission to win it. What I mean by that is they did not really prepare for what a win like that would do to their culture, infrastructure, resources, equipment load, etc. This leads up back to the discussion we started regarding being staff and service ready. But let's get to the topic at hand, onboarding clients well.

Let's assume we win the big client and we have prepared for what that means. It started during the pitch where we ended our presentation with a graphic that illustrated how we'd onboard them during the first 100 days of our partnership. This is something I have always done. Clients want to know you can handle them, regardless of the size, and they need to feel confident you will lead the process of onboarding. So, I always end my pitches with the First 100 Plan which includes getting to know their business in the way we will need to so we can be their best partner. It includes being upfront and deliberate about Ways of Working and fostering interpersonal connections between our two teams at every level. It establishes the cadence of communications and KPI tracking as well as process improvement and relationship check ins along the way. The reality is this, each partner in the relationship knows in the first 100 days if they will make it or not. A new client relationship is no different.

First 100 Days

WEEKLY GAME PLAN

MONTH 1

WK 1
A-O-R Appointment

WK 2
A-O-R Agreement signed

WK 3
Agency team assigned.
Transition meeting between
client and agency.

〉 〉 〉 〉 〉

WK 4
Vendors and media notification
of A-O-R appointment.
Immersion of new client
business.

AGENCY IMMERSION
Organization. Key practices
and processes. Plant tour.
Product review and breakouts.
Sales review. Marketing and
advertising review.

WK 5
Client and agency immersion
in ways of working.

MONTH 2

WK 6
Pre-Planning

WK 7
Planning

WK 8 - 9
Agency POV on planning
outcome.

MONTH 3

WK 10
Agency POV on planning
outcome.

WK 11 - 14
Mid- to long-term project
briefs to client.

For now, take an objective look at how your past few client onboardings went and ask yourself if you could have made them smoother. Also, if your past onboardings went well, go through the exercise of documenting what about it made it go well. Create your own First 100 Day onboarding approach and have it at the ready for your next pitch. Consider this. If your team will be engaging with young staff on the client side, I strongly encourage you to consider an in-person "get to know you" celebration of this new relationship. Once we meet people face to face, it's easier to find compassion for the mistakes we are all destined to make in the first few months. Nothing says compassion like a dose of good 'ole fashioned mixing it up.

Along with new clients often come new associates to help carry the load, and if it's a big client win, that might look like a large percentage increase in your overall staffing. A large influx of new staff can rock a culture in a good or bad way. Explore how you've done traditionally on the topic of new associate onboarding. Did you provide them enough functional training? Things like how to fill out a time sheet, how to navigate the job and traffic software you use, where the bones are buried on the server, etc. Just as important, and probably more important, did you provide a real strong understanding on the business of your client's business? The introduction of new people to an agency culture is always risky. I like to say that the only culture more emotionally volatile than an agency ecosystem is that of a kitchen at a 5-star Michelin restaurant. There is so much ego and bravado running around an agency it's easy to trip someone's trigger and the only reason the restaurant ecosystem is worse than ours is they all have knives in their hands, 😟 Seriously, we work very hard to keep the culture and vibe of our agency operating at a high functioning level and when we introduce new souls into it, well, it can get weird. So, what are you doing to ensure the onboarding of new folks will be additive and not detract from your efforts? This particular topic is one that most folks I work with have a pretty good handle on so the introspective assessment I'm asking you to do is likely not a difficult ask. That said, I would encourage you to identify that one offender in your culture that seems to protest every new addition and be mindful of the impact that is having on your efforts. It may be time for a chat or leadership training opportunity with that person. Just sayin.

Health of Your Culture

The onboarding of clients and staff is the net sum of what makes up your culture, so let's dive into that shall we? Over time I have determined that culture is a funny word for agencies. Some believe they can "create" the culture they want, others believe it's the outcome of how they lead and run the shop. The truth is, I believe these are both correct. Some will define their culture as playful and fun and be quick to point to the ping-pong table, beer tap and dog Fridays as proof. While this may very well be your shop and the table is always ping-ponging, the beer flows after hours and the dogs are welcome additions, it's not always the case. I've witnessed too many times owners who begrudgingly install all these things and then beat their team with the use of them when times get tough. Not cool, not cool at all. Others will describe their culture in more emotive ways like: we are trusting, collaborative, honest and compassionate. These tend to be the types of shops who may very well have all the trappings of a stereotypical agency and yet pay them no credit as being a contributor to their culture. Regardless of where you sit on this continuum, your culture is a reflection of you. You may have heard "you may know a kingdom by its king/queen" and, well, it's true. And that king/queen is you so get use to the idea. Oftentimes I've seen second generation owners, either children of the original or those who took over the reins of the original owners, not accepting responsibility for the state of their culture and this is a tough one to address. In those cases, there will be someone inside the shop who will take it upon themselves to shape the narrative and by extension, the culture and it may not be what you wanted. If that's you, take control of it and guide it to a new place. You owe it to everyone there.

For the most part though, when I ask agency owners how their culture is, most are enthusiastic and positive. Alas, others dip their head and admit it's strained and a bit out of control. There are all kinds of reasons for both of these scenarios and likely you know why you have the culture you have. The health and wellbeing of their culture is not always something the owners I work with are best suited to tackle themselves. Those that have figured that out have entrusted this very important role of the care and feeding of their culture to someone close to them. I'm not saying that the culture driver should NOT be the owner. Don't get me wrong, I'm saying that it does not always need to be AND furthermore, it's not always clear to the rest of the shop when it's not. That is where it can get a bit messy, but that's a story for another time. My suggestion to you is start from the highest vantage point on this topic which is to say, do you have a recognizable culture or are your team(s) simply punching the clock so to speak. If you believe you have room to improve your culture you'll want to begin to deconstruct the pieces of the everyday interactions to identify what is keeping everyone from coming together as a unified team. There are many ways to address a lackluster culture and if you are not the best suited one to take it on, make sure you are deciding who should.

"One bad apple can spoil the whole bunch." It's true and it's real. We've all seen it, we've all maybe even denied it's as bad as we think and we've all likely had to come to grips with at least one instance where it was as bad as it seemed. These culture killers, or culture culprits as I like to say, are damaging and yet, for some reason we don't always address it as we should. Now, there are a million reasons why we don't, including it could be your partner, or it could be your most productive and/or strategic associate, but no matter who it is you know you should address the situation but we don't always. As we look to our culture and assess what we have, now is the time to identify your culture culprits and make a plan on how you can address them. I'm not suggesting you get rid of them or silence their voice, I'm suggesting there may likely be underlying reasons why this individual is causing so much trouble. What I'm suggesting is that you address it with them in a way that is not threatening, yet serious. Depending on your HR practices that can mean mediation, conversation, PIP, training, etc. You know what's best, so take action because the message it's sending by not addressing it is going to continue to cause issues with the rest of the team.

Innovation and Change

Let's shift gears a bit now to the topic of innovation and change. I'm known to go on and on about how todays' innovations are tomorrows commodity and that change is a constant in our industry and that without change we will not evolve, and that if we don't embrace change and in fact seek it, we will wither on the vine and die. This is usually where one of my favorite quotes I like to use will come up. Ray Kroc, yes, that Ray Kroc was known to say "you're either green and growing or ripe and rotting." And it's so true. We are going one way or the other at all times, knowing which way you are going is not as easy as it seems. That is why I put so much emphasis on innovation which, by definition, includes change. I suppose I've always been gated for change from the very beinging of my personal life and how I grew up. You see I moved every 2-4 years most of my childhood and by the time I reached my first professional career I'd been to 8 different schools and lived from coast to coast in the U.S. When you grow up that way, change is always hanging around the next corner. So I suppose change has always been a constant for me and that served me well as I entered into leadership and ownership roles in my career. I realized that to maintain relevance we must always be taking inventory of our services and staff readiness to be considered on the leading edge of the conversation. Couple this outlook on the world with the menu/product innovation work I lead for my clients and it became second nature to insist on annual evolution of our positioning and go-to-market posture. So the question to you in all of this is, what is your tolerance for change? What is your appetite for innovation? Do you see it as a burden and something you know you need to do when pressed or do you look for windows that invite you to innovate? While there is really no right or wrong answer, I do believe you will serve your agency well if you can objectively look at yourself and how you are running your business to determine if you are future ready. If you don't believe you are, it's never too late to evolve your thinking. Last thought here for you as you assess your readiness. Remember that while necessity is the mother of invention, curiosity is the father of innovation.

The culmination of the assessment phase will reveal where you have "permission to win" and what it will take to be battle ready to fight for it.

In a traditional Observation, Implications, Opportunity strategic approach to growth strategy/platform development, it's the assessment phase which brings clarity to the overall scenario we need to understand, even if we don't like the image. It's an honest and objective perspective of the health of your agency in the context of your wants, needs and desires as the owner. Knowing where we stack up against the competition in the areas and verticals we want to work in with the team and clients we have is a liberating exercise to go through. As I've mentioned already, this assessment phase is where I begin all Growth Vision Session workshops with agency owners and principals and I have yet to reach an outcome where everyone participating did not feel more confident to make the decisions they needed to make to pursue their particular growth goals. The simple truth is this, we have a desire to be better tomorrow than we are today, however we often get sidetracked by being who we are today.

So ask yourself all those hard questions, be honest, plot out your growth goals, know where you want to be in five years and then begin to take action in the areas you know you must to get there. Easy to say, harder to do. The devil is in the details they say. Ok. Let's get into the details then.

CHAPTER 2

PREPARE

With an objective assessment fully in place, and an idea of where we want to be in 3 to 5 years, it's time to take a look at what we've got and what we need to be able to get there reasonably. I'm talking about the tools in our toolshed so to speak; everything from your web presence, awareness efforts, training and hiring strategies, to current client retention strategies and everything in between.

Now agency growth is a funny thing; oftentimes when I ask clients what are their biggest challenges relative to growth, I hear this: "we have enough calls coming in that we have never considered a new business effort." And if we're honest, that's not a bad position to be in is it? However, if we stop to consider what kind of growth we might experience if we stop responding to everything that "knocks on our door" and focused on going after the types of work we want, we might think differently about that. What I'm talking about here is the difference between reactive growth and proactive strategic growth. Consider for a minute how many requests for your time and attention you responded to in the past year. Now don't get me wrong, I'm a huge proponent of "work gets work" and that being seen in the industry as doing well for a brand/company is the best adverting we have in the agency business. However, I'm suggesting that anyone can, and often will, request your time and talent for their brand. And why not?

If you had the opportunity wouldn't you approach the very best in the business to work on your account? Well that is often the case with clients who approach us for a bid or proposal. While it's satisfying to know that we are "wanted" it's less fulfilling to learn they have very small budgets, are not sophisticated in the ways of marketing/communications and will require double the time to earn half the fee. This is not a margin building proposition and yet, we say yes too often to the these inquiries for our time and talent because well, they asked. Now consider all the time that you spent answering all those requests and how many good clients came out of that. Oftentimes when I speak with agency ownership what I hear is that they are so busy responding to requests for RFI's or RFP's or even a competitive pitch scenario, that they always seem to be involved in a pitch. What makes it hard, is that they're not winning very many of them. Or, even worse to some degree, is that they are winning them, yet they are not profitable accounts or projects. Neither of these scenarios are good, nor should it be your strategy for growth. STOP. There is an alternative, and that is to identify who we work well with, the types of industries and business verticals you want to work inside and spend the time to develop, and the positioning to attract the right clients inside those industries. In short, defining the landscape of where you have "permission to win" and defining the targets inside that landscape. Take charge of your agency growth destiny and begin to identify those clients you want to work with, those who you believe will continue to see value in your expertise and perspectives and, most importantly, those who your team want to work with.

Now the preparations begin. Let's start with your front door, or your *virtual* front door to be more exact, your website. One hundred percent of all agency searches begin with a visit to the website. What is your website saying? Have you declared your specialty or focus on your landing page? Do you make it easy for people to contact you through the website? Have you highlighted your best work or all of your work?

The thing about agency websites is, we can get caught up showing pictures of our dog Fridays or our ping-pong table culture and not enough about our expertise. Now, don't get me wrong here, I love dogs at the office and am a ping-pong fanatic, however, it's not what we should lead with on our websites. While it's important to let folks know who you are and your personality, it's infinitely more important to let them know where your expertise lies. The more specific and deliberate you can get delivering your expertise, the better off you are. I have had agency owners tell me they're cautious about being too narrowly focused. I would suggest that you can never be too narrowly focused. If you become the only agency on the planet to declare a specialty in a specific area, the odds of you receiving 100% of the work in that area are pretty high. Think of it this way, prospects will be prequalified by the time they actually talk to you if they understand where your areas of expertise lie. You won't waste time trying to explain exactly what it is you can do for them. Think about how focused you can be driving people to the website to learn about your expertise. This realization should be liberating, not anxiety producing. Remember your competition is stiff enough, why not create as much distance between you and them as you can every chance you get? And that starts with a very dialed in positioning and web presence.

Let's focus now on how we get people to our website. We are experts when it comes to driving customers to our clients site or location, but why not ours? Let's build the kind of content that intrigues our target to the degree that they want to know more. We have already mentioned the value of being "IN" the conversation and even more powerful, to be leading the conversation of your focused vertical. Now is the time to leverage that. Consider the journey your prospects take to find the best marketing communications partner. Now, let's be at every step along the way with provocative content that leads them to your site. This path likely meanders through the industry, past the trade associations and directly into their customers domain; let's be sure we are intersecting them at every turn.

Preparation goes well beyond the website, software and a robust CRM. It must include the readiness of your staff or it's all for naught. I've seen it too often; an agency is all in on a proactive strategically grounded growth effort including aggressive prospecting and constant industry awareness, yet does nothing to train up their team to be ready to handle the flood of work. It's truly heartbreaking to see the efforts of the business development team be stifled by an ill-prepared team. We have all seen this if we stay around the agency business long enough.

The narrative goes something like this. Agency leadership has been hard at work. They've identified their prospects, they've updated their website and have engaged in the conversation of the industries they want to focus on. They've engaged in a robust and sophisticated CRM platform that will allow them to generate inbound and outbound content in the way that they can track it, follow up, and measure success. Their content calendar is in perfect sync with the conversation of the industry, and they have absolutely killer content they're turning out. The response is fantastic, the prospect pipeline is full, and the connections and invitations to present capabilities are flowing like never before. Their current clients are engaged in seeing the value in what they have to offer in terms of the content they are putting out, and the competition is wondering what's going on. And then it hits, invitations to engage in formal RFI's, RFP's and pitches are coming at them like gangbusters. They're engaging in just the top opportunities, which is great, and ,in fact, winning. Winning the right new clients, the ones that they had on their radar, the ones that they were going after. By all accounts this is textbook; the exact right way to go about strategically growing your agency. There is only one problem. They did not take seriously the need to train the staff to be equipped to handle the amount or depth of work.

You see, while leadership was confident, engaged, aggressive and committed, they were the only one capable of having the conversations and thus, once the work came in, their incredible business engine came to a screeching halt because they had to go work the new clients. What a disastrous interruption to success!

So, let's break this down and look at all the areas we need to focus on to truly be prepared to go prospect.

CHAPTER 3

CORE AGENCY FOCUS

When I ask agencies about their core focus, I get one of two responses. Either they describe a specific business category such as healthcare or food/beverage or they describe a function such as branding, digital or PR. I'll suggest that if you are in the latter description category as to what your core focus is, you have an opportunity to identify what business category or business channel you want to focus your functional energy. You may be thinking, "Well, I do identify my focus as the function but that's because my focus is my market". OK. I get that as well, but I'm still challenging you to declare a channel or business focus. The reason is this, when we compete in a market using our functional services as the lead discussion, we are more likely to have a price driven discussion than if we were to lead with our declared expertise focus.

Now, I realize it's a decent size leap I'm asking you to make here but stick with me. Getting to expert levels don't happen overnight and likely take years to perfect, so if you are evolving from a function first positioning, let's start with experience over function and work toward expertise. Take a look at your work over the past three years and be honest about the categories you enjoyed working in the most, where the real passion is, and start there. If you've worked in that category over the past three years, you have experience there and that is the platform from which to launch expertise.

If you have a declared business category as your focus or maybe even two, that's fantastic. Let's turn your preparation challenge to refining that even further. For example, if you have declared your focus area to be travel and leisure, put a finer point on that and determine what communications aspects of that category you are most knowledgeable in; advertising, PR, social, influencer, digital, etc. Start with your strongest tool and work to fill in the rest as you expand through talent acquisition and training.

Experience vs Expertise

Let's get back to this notion that expertise is the long game and it begins with experience. To be seen as an expert in a category of business is no small challenge and one that will have some folks laughing when you profess your expertise in their category. I'm not suggesting we outwardly profess our expertise, but rather conduct our agency as such, expressed by the caliber of our content and ability to navigate the conversation of the industries we serve. When we are seen as a credible source of information in a business category, others will refer to your agency as the experts in the business category you chose. This does not mean we become experts in hospitality or food and beverage but rather the experts at navigating the landscape of their business from a strategic marketing and communications or brand positioning perspective. Remember, they are in the hotel or spaghetti business, not necessarily the marketing business. That's our end of the field as their trusted partner and we definitely must understand the business of their business if we are to be elevated to this level. When our clients are asking us to participate in their strategic planning and/or write their plan, you know you have achieved this level. If you have never been asked to participate, work to find a way to bring value to the planning conversation and push for involvement. You'll be delighted with the new lens your client sees you through. And that is achieving expertise in the eyes of the category.

How to Conduct a Conversation Audit

We've referred to the conversation audit a few times thus far, so let's get into it. The conversation of the industries we choose to work in is simply the way I refer to the main discussion topics, pain points, trends, news, innovations, concerns, roadblocks, public opinions, quantified facts, etc. These are the same contributors to virtually any conversation. I used to say, "For $50 in magazine subscriptions I can become conversant in any topic, from needlepoint to aeronautical engineering." Nothing has changed in that regard, expect that now it's free, broader and deeper and at our fingertips for the taking.

It's important to understand and be able to identify the conversation in the industries we want to work in because this is how we can add value to the clients we serve in that industry/vertical as well as how we begin to identify the opportunity areas for us to enter through. Think of it this way, when going to a first meeting with a prospect we want to be prepared right? (Don't answer that unless it's yes). How do we get prepared? There are a lot of ways to get to know the company, the brand, the leaders, what makes them news worthy, etc. If you are like most folks today, you start by Googling the company, click on their website, cruise around in there for a while and then back to the Google results to see what else you can read about them. You might also go onto LinkedIn to see if you can find the leaders and read up on them as well. And finally, you might inquire with trusted friends to find out what they know about them. All these are the intuitive ways we might prepare to meet a new prospect for the first time. And why? So that we can have a conversation with them about their business backed by fact and observation. I'm suggesting the same approach here, but simply backing up one step to understand more about the category/vertical as a whole before we dig into specific companies and brands (we'll get to that in the prospecting chapter).

Keeping with this line of thinking and approach, we can correlate our search for the category/vertical conversation just the way we do for a company. I like to start at the highest point of this diagram so instead of Googling a company, we Google the category/vertical and seek out the associations that support them.

Conversation Audit

THE INDUSTRY

Industry associations
Leading industry publications
Leading industry influencers/innovators
Industry trends
Industry innovations/inventions
Industry data and insights
Industry legislation

CONVERSATION AUDIT

OBSERVATION

IMPLICATION

OPPORTUNITY

WHITE PAPER

OUTBOUND EMAIL CAMPAIGN

Remember, I've mentioned that there are associations for practically anything you can think of so start there because they are often the most objective source of information. Next, search for and identify the trade shows and conventions that support those associations and their members. Put those aside, we'll come back to those soon. Now, identify the trade publications/digital resources that report on that category/vertical and pull up the past six months' worth of published materials for your research. Put those aside. Identify the trade shows and conventions/summits these publishing arms support and bookmark those sites. Lastly, identify any experts publishing on the topic from the past six months and hold on to them. Now we have assembled quite a nice collection of fact and opinion and it's time to digest the information to identify the conversation(s) being had in that category/vertical. I like to look over the syllabus and speaker lineup for the events regardless of who is putting on the event. This goes for association meetings, conventions, trade shows, summits, etc. Once you pull the agendas/syllabus for these events and begin to compare topics you'll quickly identify a trend in these topics. You'll likely see some similar, if not the same, speakers supporting these agendas as well. While this may seem intuitive, the practice of it is rarely completed. If you have been involved in a particular industry category/vertical for a long time, you are likely one of the speakers who is asked to present on particular topics. Which is the goal of industry involvement and one which we will get to later in the book. For now, let's stay on the conversation and how to identify and leverage it.

Now that we have collected the discussion topics from a variety of sources involved in the industry of choice, it's time to assemble a Top Topics list for deeper understanding and observation. The goal is to identify where you can jump into the conversation and be believable. This will also inform your inbound and outbound content creation platforms and speaking/publishing platforms as we dive further into the industry events ourselves. You see, the conversation is very important to understand if we want to shift our experience to expertise and be seen as the type of partner who can add value to the business of our client's business. The success of leveraging the conversation has proven out time and time again regardless of the industry, from food/drink, to healthcare, to hospitality, to financial services, to wherever you have permission to lean in. It's just smart strategy.

Now, getting to the useful part of the conversation, that which we can leverage to promote awareness of our agency among prospects in that category, I like to follow a simple Observation, Implication, Opportunity strategic path to help frame up the platforms for content creation. It's a way to pressure test our "permission to win" in the conversation. Do we truly have anything to say that adds value to the topics? Start there to begin to frame up your content calendar. Oh, and don't discard any of the resources you've pulled just yet, you'll need the calendars and timing of the conversations happening in the industry to choreograph your own awareness campaign efforts to ensure you are taking advantage of every aspect of the timing of that topic. We'll get into that more in the prospecting chapter.

What's Your Client Retention Strategy?

While we know the best new business prospect is our existing clients, we sometimes act like they'll be here forever and how we engage with them will always be how we engage with them. Well, I don't believe either of those "hopes" are particularly wise to bank on, nor do I think they are true.

There are certain proactive actions we can take with our current clients to help ensure we are staying relevant and valuable to them. Regardless of the size of the client, the following are basic block and tackle account management activities which can help do just that, retain them.

- Annual business reviews. Once per year it's appropriate to have a meeting about the business of your relationship. This is the time to celebrate the wins, discuss the losses, brainstorm the future and concede the commoditized services. What I mean by looking at the business of the relationship means it's time to determine if the agreement and ways of working with this client are working for you. Are you making the margin you should on the work you do? Is the work good? Are there services your client continues to request from you at a rate you cannot make money on? Are there services you offer other clients which you believe this client can benefit from? The annual business review is the time to cover all of this and more. It's important that your clients understand that you are consistently innovating on their behalf, take the lead in this conversation and show them how you propose to lead the relationship more efficiently.
- Proactive initiative thinking. I have not met a client yet that did not appreciate initiative thinking they did not ask for, yet we stopped doing it somewhere around 2000. I don't know what happened, but it just sort of dried up. One of the top reasons a client will fire an agency is because they are not bringing them new thinking. I know there are a million reasons why we don't do this on a regular basis, and they are all time related,

but that has to change if you want to do everything you can to maintain your relevance and have permission to ask for more.

- Cross train/pollinate the account with new associates. Three things happen when you make this a policy at your shop.
  - Your clients receive new thinking and perspectives to help keep the work fresh
  - You allow associates to continue their personal growth path by exposing them to different clients
  - You as the owner, insulate yourself from the risk of having the account be dependent on one person/relationship

One way we can address two of these client retention strategies is to institute an initiative plan for each client 2x/year. The basics of how to action this include:

- Identify a mix of associates from different teams to work on an initiative for a client they don't normally work on.
- Make observations about what's happening in the client's industry and propose an opportunity to take advantage of what's happening. Write the brief and have the sitting account leader approve it.
- Have the team present the work to the sitting team leaders as a way to ensure the thinking is on brand and in line with client goals.
- Have the sitting client lead arrange for this cross functional team to present the thinking to the client.

Two things will happen.

1. Client will be pleased to see the attention they are getting and will credit their sitting agency lead with the initiative.
2. The client will now be introduced to others at the agency. This is a good thing because there are times when current team members my need to take a leave or decide to move on. When that happens we are often left flat footed as to who we replace them with. Not anymore. The relationship has already begun with the new team members.

I think we can all see the value in this sort of cross functional initiative thinking. I can attest to this approach. It's invigorating for the current team and those you invite in to help see it from a new perspective.

CHAPTER 4

UNIQUE SELLING
PROPOSITION/POSITIONING

We do this work for our clients every day, now It's time to put your agency through your own process; and you know you have one, even if it's not published. For some smaller shops the selling proposition is a very fluid statement, something that is not necessarily identified as the selling proposition but rather, their "approach." For larger and/or more formal shops this is a statement that is consternated over, discussed and cussed and often left to a copywriter to articulate because the committee of input that created it has it sounding like they solve world hunger. Now, I'm not poking fun at either of these scenarios, heck I've participated in both along the way, I'm simply saying that there is a need to know and be able to communicate what your selling proposition is or you will be vacillating on emotion rather than vetted commitment. Identifying your selling proposition includes pushing the discussion far enough to make it a unique selling proposition. Here is the definition once again as a reminder.

A **unique selling proposition** is a factor that differentiates a product from its competitors, such as the lowest cost, the highest quality or the first-ever product of its kind. A **USP** could be thought of as "what you have that competitors don't."

If you have never put your agency through the exercise to determine what your USP is, now is the time. I like to include the discussion of your value proposition in this context to ensure you are landing on a selling proposition that is based in value, not function.

The same holds true for understanding your positioning. How you will articulate your USP and Value Proposition to the world will depend largely on your positioning. You'll want to be sure your positioning in and among your competitive set gives your agency enough latitude to traverse all the corners of the categories you want to compete in. Consider how your outward positioning is received by the different categories/verticals you want to compete it. You'll dig into this more in the next section on Strategic Adjacencies.

Strategic Adjacencies

We have our core categories/verticals we work in on a day to day basis and we have the natural extension of that work into adjacent categories/verticals. Consider for a moment an agency that focuses on the foodservice vertical as it's main category. The adjacent categories to the foodservice vertical include food processing and ingredients further down the chain and restaurants and grocery channels further up the chain. Take a look at where you spend your time, what target audience you would consider yourselves experts in understanding and determine what other purchase or decision making insights you have about that audience. The categories/verticals that target engages in is likely a viable strategic adjacency for you to consider.

Another way to identify where you have "permission to win," and thus, prospect in that category/vertical, is by deconstructing your Unique Selling Proposition and Value Proposition. By breaking down what you do for your clients, and where the value lies, you can identify other growth pillars to consider.

Identify Your White Space: Where Can You Go, Where Should You Go

While retention of current clients should be Job No. 1, it goes hand in hand with identifying white space or opportunity growth space to continue your market and/or channel expansion.

You will recall from the assessment phase the talent and service audit we discussed. The outcome of that exercise will help inform not only where you can go, but also, where you should go.

Draw on your Marketing 101 training to help guide your thinking here. Meaning, consider the following inputs to reveal where your agency can and should go:

- Current staff and their abilities
- Current service offerings and level of experience in those areas
- Current channels and verticals you work in today
- Strategic adjacencies to those channels and verticals where you have "permission to win"
- Current competitive landscape in your core and strategic adjacencies. I recommend a plotting exercise here as we discussed in the assessment phase.
- Specific company and brand conflicts you may have. (Note, your incumbent clients will be the ones calling foul on conflict so put yourself in their shoes when determining this).
- State of the industry at the moment. I like to conduct what I call a "category physical." Think of

this as taking the temperature of the channel/vertical you are considering and be realistic about what you find there. If they are having a COVID-19 breakout, pass on it for now. Consider the following to analyze during your category physical:

- o Size of the category/vertical (dollar, players, % share by top brands, geographic penetration, etc)
- o Top 5-10 companies/brands dominating that category/vertical and % share and dollar for each
- o Recent innovation in the category/vertical
- o Leading innovators in that category/vertical
- o Projection of potential growth based on current economic indicators
- o Any recent mergers or acquisitions by key players
- o List of next 50 brands in the channel/category: name, HQ location, % market share if possible, strengths, recent new products/innovation and anything else that makes sense for the category such as recent patents, awards, new land purchases, etc.
- o Key associations and events/shows/conventions supporting the category/vertical
- o Initial Observation, Implication, Opportunity assessment of the this category/vertical
- Relevant case studies supporting expertise/experience in the category/vertical

- Identify any other revenue generating opportunities you have inside your shop that you have not considered before. For example, your facility may be equipped with an industrial kitchen because you conduct food and menu R&D as part of your daily work for clients. That is an asset you may consider using in other ways. Get creative about considering how that kitchen can earn your agency revenue when not in use. There are many examples like this and frankly, you may be employing someone who has the passion and energy to take on such a challenge as this.

The whole idea here is to identify categories and industry verticals where you have "permission to win." The difference between where you can go and where you should go lies mainly in your ability to penetrate the category/vertical and gain new clients. The final vetting of your white space growth opportunities may very well be a ranking of where you should start and allow those to be your should(s). Consider as well, the investment it will take to engage in these white space growth opportunities and be real about your resourcing to see it done.

CHAPTER 5

PROSPECTING STRATEGY

An important part of our preparation before we begin to actively pursue prospects is to be sure our strategy is sound. While this is of course a no-brainer, oftentimes I work with folks who want to jump in both feet first with an action plan that has no backbone/strategy. So let's do this. We know what our objective is: to <u>gain new clients</u>, so what do you believe the strategy to accomplish this might look like? We took a look earlier in the book at the choreography of a potential growth trajectory and that certainly is a good place to start. The strategy, which lies in that choreography, is the way we build our credibility and expertise. We create a culture of growth; a culture which equips us with what we need for "permission to win." Simply put, your prospecting strategy is to <u>become focused and intentional on preparing your agency to always be in a posture of growth</u>. What this looks like is to honestly and objectively assess where you are, prepare your agency and arm it with what you need to generate awareness among your target and have a team ready to handle it when the work comes in. Then go out into the industry categories/verticals of your clients and be the voice leading the conversation. Simple, right? 😌

Prospecting Action Plan

The action plan for our prospecting efforts is a bit more academic. In fact ,I've boiled it down to these simple models. Begin with identifying what your content will be based on the conversation audit you have completed. Identify the target personas you want to reach and create an editorial calendar to keep you on track. Your calendar should correlate to the industry events and conversations happening at those events.

You can look at this preparation in three phases:

1. Content and target database development
2. Strategic deployment and tracking/follow up
3. Initial client engagement

Content Calendar Distillation

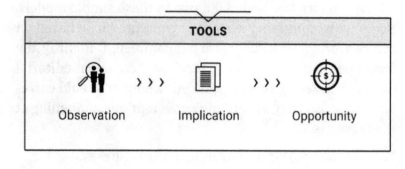

TOOLS

Observation > > > Implication > > > Opportunity

Conversation driven content!

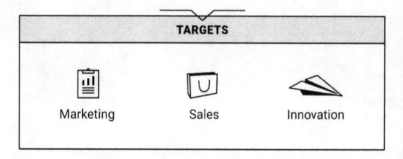

TARGETS

Marketing   Sales   Innovation

ROLLING CALENDAR

MTH 1	MTH 2	MTH 3	MTH 4
1, 2, 3, 4	5, 6, 7, 8	9, 10 1, 2, 3, 4	5, 6, 7, 8

3 Phase Approach

PHASE 1

CONTENT DEVELOPMENT

DATABASE DEVELOPMENT

CRM INTEGRATION

PHASE 2

STRATEGIC DEPLOYMENT

TRACKING & MEASUREMENT

FOLLOW THROUGH

PHASE 3

ENGAGEMENT

Materials/Support/Tools

You'll need to be ready to respond to the new client activity you will generate and now is the time to take an inventory on your readiness. Here's the checklist:

- Website updated to reflect USP, positioning and relevant to the prospects you are going after. Remember, your website is a business development tool, be sure that is the filter you use as you update/build it. What it's not is a recruitment tool or trophy case.
- Conversation audit completed and relevant topics identified for content creation
- Content calendar synced up with the industry events
- Prospect database curated and loaded into CRM (or at least under way; the list curation can take some time)
- CRM set up and ready to receive inbound inquiries as well as send outbound emails
- Follow up template concepted and designed
- Industry events prioritized, budgeted and scheduled
- Initiative protocol in place
- Social media platforms updated and populated
- Training regimen in place

Growth Strategies

Lastly, as we wrap up our preparation, the reminder of our growth strategies; those which lead to informing your specific growth platforms.

- Protect and expand your core. Are you prepared to implement what it will take to do this?

- Identify strategic adjacencies. Are you confident with where you have "permission to win"? This includes the ideal client persona you will pursue.
- Innovate to win. Have you carefully considered what your service and talent audit told you? Do you know where you need to innovate? Where you need to update and where you need to concede?
- Awareness and exposure. Have you identified how you will introduce yourself to your prospects, what you will lead with and how you will position your agency to them?

CHAPTER 6

PROSPECTING

The success of your prospecting effort is predicated on what you have to offer to your audience. Understanding the "conversation" of the focus vertical you're working in, is just as important as curating your database with the right targets. As a reminder, to identify the conversation of any industry, start with an observation of the topics which seem to continue to be highlighted in articles of trade magazines, agenda items at trade conferences and events, and the discussions your clients are having in their executive boardrooms. It's the new legislation, or new flavor trend, health trend, safety trend, labor issues, tariffs, and a thousand other topics that make up what we talk about in the industries we work in. As with any conversation, there's a point of entry that makes sense for any participant to join in with their opinion and thoughts. Identifying that entry point and having something valuable to add, is key to carving out your platform for generating awareness and interest in your particular area of expertise and value you offer to clients.

A fine way to test out your hypothesis on this conversation entry point is with current clients in that vertical. In the context of an initiative meeting, frame up your observations of the conversation in a way that adds value to your clients challenges and/or goals. You'll find out soon enough whether or not there is true value in your perspective or rather simply an observation. I like to frame this initiative strategy in a simple approach outline. One which is easy to accept and digest by clients and clear on the desired action. It is one thing to have an opinion on a major topic in the industry, it is alltogether more provocative to have an initiative to propose for consideration. The simple framework of this approach outlines as such:

1. Observation
2. Implication
3. Opportunity

Where to look to identify the "conversation" of your focused vertical? While intuitive to some, it's a mystery to others so I thought I'd sketch out where to look to get a handle on what matters to your clients and prospective clients. I usually start with the trade publications (print and on-line), even if you are working in a consumer facing industry, because the "issues" of the industry are not always apparent to the end users (consumers) but they are what drive decision making inside that industry. From there I'll scour the internet for articles, blog posting, pod-casts and other open forums on the topic. These usually center around the association(s) of that industry (remember to consider the many congruent associations which may be intertwined with the industry to get the whole picture). Go deep up and down the go-to-market channel to get a broad understanding of the industry and its driving topics. Look for signs of seasonality, regionality, social/political triggers and how pop culture plays into the tenor of the conversation. There is something very important to be noted by considering the tenor of the conversation in context of the current social/political climate. What was once a "non-issue" or "non-opportunity" may now be the biggest threat or blue ocean opportunity to consider in the industry and you don't want to miss it because it was previously considered an industry standard. Think about the issues that were important to the hospitality industry pre-COVID-19 pandemic of 2020 and what is important to them now.

Whether you have been in the industry you have chosen as your focused vertical for one or two years or one month, identifying the conversation is not difficult, it simply takes purpose driven digging to uncover it. I will also suggest that if you have been working in an industry for more than three years and you have not reassessed the conversation of that vertical, it's probably time to do so. Remember, perspectives, like ideas, are perishable and they must be constantly refreshed and evolved.

Once you are confident you have identified the conversation, and have been proactive with your current clients on how to best navigate action for success/growth in that industry with this understanding, it's time to take it to the prospects. Creating a cadence with your prospects is key to delivering on the notion of expertise. Imagine, if you will, that everything you published or used as your platform for generating awareness was simply an observation of the conversation being had by others. Wouldn't that fall a bit flat on the value spectrum? If, however, your observation, implication and opportunity approach landed your agency on the forefront of industry insight that drove growth, wouldn't that be something others might like to benefit from? This is the core of a successful new business approach in a deliberate business development discipline. It's what elevates your agency from experience in a vertical, to being the expert in that vertical. To best leverage these insights, we must look at all the communication triggers in the industry and integrate into their cadence. What I mean by that is simply this, most trade publications/websites have an editorial calendar that is published at least six months out so we as advertisers know when to run our best matched product/service ads to match the articles. Likewise, most trade events have their agenda/syllabus published six months out as well. These are the two main conversation indicators to any industry.

Obtain these calendars and overlay those with your outbound awareness effort and be sure to have an opinion/insight on these topics prior to the published versions by the industry trade. You'll create the type of thought leadership that clients are looking for by being ahead of the conversation, or at least in tune with it.

One of my favorite ways to engage in the conversation at a trade event is by gap filling against the syllabus or agenda with the obvious missed topic angle to the conversation. For example, let's say you are planning to attend the big annual industry trade association conference and of course you check out the agenda to make sure you are prepared with your conversation talking points. On that agenda are the usual suspects, meaning, all the usual industry expert speakers including topic areas you would expect to be covered by the industry such as updates, initiatives, trends, tips on how to adjust to changes affecting the industry, etc. What you do not see anywhere is the glaring and/or controversial topics you know are on everyone's mind and lips. You don't see these types of topics there for good reason; remember, this association is funded by membership and sponsorship. Covering "said" topic would cause conflict and discord among supporters and funding agents (these events are for-profit ventures and big ones at that). That's where you come in. Tackle this missed and possible controversial topic in a way that allows you to maintain an objective perspective yet provide advice and guidance on how to *navigate* it regardless of which side of the issue one might find themselves. We are in the communications business and we must be able to address any issue a client is facing. Not to mention we must be in tune with the business of our clients business to the degree that we understand what they are up against in their own industry.

To create a meaningful mini-event to engage in the conversation at this level at the largest industry gathering of the year takes confidence and preparation. The right venue, the right speakers, the right value proposition and positioning of the narrative is key to attracting the right attendees. The cadence of the conversation is real and the weeks leading up to the event is a very important time to be communicating your intent and expectation of your gathering. Ultimately, the mini-event you will hold during an annual conference will be the live version of the event you have been promoting for the past weeks and will allow attendees to engage in an important aspect of their industry, and more importantly, one that is not covered by the event host. The goal is an inclusive exclusive event attended by thought leaders in the industry to engage in an important topic to the industry and by extension, all their businesses. Be the host agency that brought this important conversation to the forefront. What better way to demonstrate your level of expertise in not only the industry and it's challenges but also in communications expertise.

Addressing the topics no one else wants to tackle is one of my favorite things to do and certainly has been a catalyst to engaging targeted prospects with the agencies I work with in a way that sets them far above their competition who rented booth space or sponsored a break. While you don't want to make an enemy of the event host, you do want to be bold in your resolve to address the topic/issue, so be sure to plan accordingly.

The best way to get noticed is to create a non-competing VIP mini-event alongside/inside the main event timing. Host an early evening cocktail event or even an evening event during the open night of the conference and invite a list of hand-picked prospects to attend. Promoting the event is key to its success. Start six weeks out from the big day by sending targeted communications to generate awareness and interest around the topic among the personas on your profile target list within the right brands. Create such an event that it will be the talk of the show and one that will set you leaps and bounds above your competitive set. Don't be afraid to bring in a key note or celebrity author or expert on the topic who is open to telling it like it is. Get the conversation moving in a new direction, this is where your agency will cross over from being involved in the conversation to leading the conversation. A very powerful growth point in an agencies path to achieving expertise status to be certain.

Chapter 7

Outbound

Thus far there has been a lot of planning, a lot of strategy to consider, a lot to rework or create and, at times, it may have seemed you would never be ready to launch your first campaign. Alas, you are there. This process to this point usually takes agencies I work with three months (minimum). While we identify and believe we can be ready in 60 days, there is always something that crops up to throw a wrench into that plan (it's usually the website revision). With your tools sharpened so to speak, and your target audience identified, a list of them curated and loaded into your CRM, and all the other preparation details attended to, you are ready to begin the inbound/outbound flow of content needed to generate the awareness you need to be considered for engagement. It all comes down to this as they say.

Be prepared to learn a lot on your first deployment of an outbound campaign, not the least of which is that more of your list than you expected is bouncing back for some reason. Not to worry, clean it out, keep it clean, and continue to add new contacts to it over time. The other thing you may find is that you are not getting the open or click rate you want on the first few campaign deployments. Again, not to worry, it takes time for someone you don't know to see enough from you to entice them to open the email; just think of your own in-box. It has been my experience that somewhere around the third to fifth e-mail in a campaign, the open and clicks seem to begin to pick up. Be patient, don't be discouraged. Remember, this is a long game strategy and the sooner you dive in the sooner it begins to take hold. Which reminds me; if by this point you have not shifted your thinking that "new business" is the result of a well thought out strategic business development plan and not something you can turn on and off, I'd suggest you go back to the beginning of the book and start over.

The E-mail Campaign

It's time to write those e-mails and you may be struggling with this a bit. Is e-mail marketing dead, how long should it be, how "salesy" should it be, how much do I need to convey in each e-mail, etc.? I generally get a lot of questions about this step in the process. The short answer is this: be clear on the objective of the e-mail before you sit down to write the copy. And, the objective is simple, remember this is an awareness campaign, not a sales promotion. If you expect your audience to receive this well-crafted e-mail and call you with a project, you will be disappointed. They will not. What you are attempting to do is generate awareness among a very specific group of targeted prospects in a way that positions you as a viable partner for their marketing/branding/advertising/communications needs. That's it. So the objective of the outbound e-mail is to entice them to click over to your site to learn more about you. You don't have to give it all away in the e-mail either. There is power in being brief. Give enough to establish your position and expertise yet not so much that it's a commitment to read through it. Remember, these are first impressions and you plan to provide many more. There is time for the relationship to form. Also, you'll want to take the topic of the e-mail and have a deeper dive perspective written and ready to go in the form of a good 'ole fashioned white paper or opinion paper. This is what we'll send anyone who opens and clicks over to learn more about you. It is also the execution of the particular topic/content that will live on your site later for inbound prospects to find.

Monitoring

While your e-mail campaign is live and going (e-blasts, social posting, inbound coming into the CRM), be sure you are monitoring the activity not only inside your CRM but also each social platform and your website. Regardless of how big you are, 13 or 300, creating a dashboard is a good idea. It does not need to be anything elaborate, however, it should be tracking the KPI's that are important to you. Here is a sample dashboard we created for a group that happened to be in the credit union vertical so it was important to them to see where their traffic was coming in from.

Outbound Awareness

EFFORT + FOLLOW THRU = EARNINGS

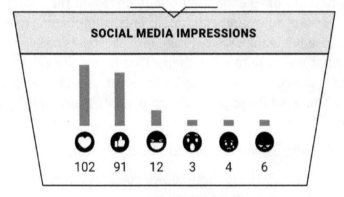

OUTBOUND CAMPAIGN STATISTICS

Opens	Click Throughs	Meeting Requests
1,470	548	6

SOCIAL MEDIA IMPRESSIONS

102	91	12	3	4	6

KPI'S

List Size Increases	32
New Meetings	5
Proposals	4
Projects	2
Earnings	**$$$**

We all understand the benefits of tracking and reporting on our activity so keep this in mind when you kick off your own campaign. You'll be glad you have it later.

Follow Up

Once you begin to see the open rates increase and you are beginning to drive traffic to your site, it's time to follow up with these prospects so let's be sure we have something of value to offer them when we reach out to them in follow up. One piece of valuable content we just talked about was the need to have expanded perspectives on the topics we use for our outbound campaign. This is important to have because we want to encourage our prospects to see value in what we have to offer them. This is the close-in extension of the conversation topics/content and it has a second use. These white papers will be used as training for your team.

Think of the conversation audit being leveraged as follows:

- Identify the leading topics you'll use as content for your awareness campaign.
  - First use of this information will be the brief overview of your observation, implication and opportunity insights in the way of an outbound e-mail for the campaign.
- Second will be a deeper dive into this in the form of a white paper we'll use as follow up content for our active prospects who show interest in that topic.
- The same white paper will later become part of our library of insight on your website (after it has been used as follow up for your outbound campaign).

- Third, this white paper will be turned into a training module you can use to train up your team on the very specific topics you are going out into the industry with as a calling card. This will help ensure you are entering the conversations of the industry with one united and confident voice.
  - Lastly, this white paper can be used as a tool to engage industry show organizers on how you would create a breakout or workshop session for their attendees at the next gathering.

Net, net, once the conversation has been identified and the content has been created, be sure you are leveraging it to the fullest. It will not last forever, it is perishable, so be sure it feeds as many purposes as it can while it's relevant.

Prospecting does not start and end with an e-mail campaign bolstered up by white papers and podcasts; no, that's simply the beginning. Consider your prospecting effort to be something that's on your mind and being promoted all the time. If you get creative with all the ways you can leverage your content you'll see the avenues to introduce your agency to even more qualified prospects seems almost limitless. But in case you were looking for a few thought starters, here you go. These are some of the avenues you should consider leveraging your content in beyond outbound e-mail and white papers:

- Blogs
- Podcasts
- Panel discussions
- Breakout sessions at existing industry events
- Client specific lunch and learns
- Training excursions where you can interact with the content of the topic firsthand (also provides another opportunity to capture this excursion in video format and share even more)

- Research primer
- Publishing (book, e-zine, etc.)
- University and other continued-education lectures
- Radio show appearances
- Talk show appearances
- Short film
- Social media short clip videos
- Event theme
- Case study development
- And so many more.

The reality is that prospecting is a full time job for the right person. There are so many ways to leverage your content if only you have the focus and diligence it takes to bring these types of opportunities to fruition.

Industry Involvement

One very important aspect of prospecting is the face to face interaction that happens during industry events, which holds true even if face to face is virtual. Even though we will not always attend or engage in person, the philosophical approach to industry involvement holds true.

Regardless of whether you are attending, speaking, keynoting, working a booth or auditing an event, there are ways to make sure you are being introduced to your target in the way you want to be received. Now, there are several kinds of events and they are not all created equally. There are trade shows, conventions, summits, conferences, association meetings, etc. and the objective for attendance at each differs. For example:

> ➤ Trade Show: is all about making personal connections to the brand and folks in the booth and collecting intelligence from the vast array of other brands participating in the show.

> ➤ Conference: Do all you can to be part of the conversation. Attend the breakouts, ask smart questions of the speakers, be seen engaging in the conversation.
> ➤ Association Event: Go with your clients and do all you can to connect them with prospects. Serve on a committee/board and engage in that way.

Regardless of the type of event, be enthusiastic about being there and meet as many people as you can.

Once you've made the financial and time commitment to attend an event, regardless of what kind it is, be sure you are getting everything out of it you can. Now, we've likely all had good intention to meet the "right" folks at the event, but simply ran out of time before the event to set something up for an introduction. "No worries" you think, "I'll just go and see who I can run into." How many times have we said this (way too many for me) and that's when we stopped. We have a responsibility to the rest of our company to be as efficient with our time and resources as possible and that means making sure we have a plan when we attend these events. That's when I pulled together a training module for my team that helped guide the preparation as well as calibrate expectations and it all begins one month out from the first day of the event. Remember, industry involvement is one of the four key pillars to a successful Business Development approach and that means it is part of this discussion. Let's break it down by week from one month out:

Week 4: Register and determine your approach

Week 3: Identify attendees, prioritize your targets and make a list/map the show for efficiency (in the case of a trade show with booths)

Week 2: Send initial outreach to your full target list

Week 1: Resend outreach to all those who have not responded

Week of the event: Have your plan ready, have something to share and keep your eyes open

Determining your approach. Depending on the type of event it is will help shape your approach. If it's a trade show, you'll know exactly where your prospects are..... they're in their booth. If it's a conference or summit it's a bit more difficult to find them. Although you might be lucky and find that one of your top prospects is speaking at a breakout, moderating a panel or in some way on the agenda. You'll know exactly when and where they'll be, so you can be there as well. Be realistic about what you can accomplish in the atmosphere of an event. Beyond introductions and making a first impression there really is not much more you can do. Unless of course you are on the agenda in some way. So, be realistic, you will not be flipping open your laptop to give a capabilities presentation on the trade show floor. You may laugh, but I've had to explain this to more than one person. We've talked about mini events inside the event for your top prospects. If this is something you are committed to doing, the rest of the planning time should be used to coordinate that. If not, keep going.

Identify and connect with your prospect before the event dates. Because we have done the work to identify our perfect client, including bracketing them by certain criteria, we know who we want to meet at the event. For example, your criteria for the perfect client might look like this:

> ➢ Do they operate inside our core or one of our strategic adjacencies?

> Can we work with them (meaning, do we have any conflicts)?

> Budget of at least $250,000 AOR/project?

> Do we have "permission to win" with them (do we have expertise to offer them)?

> Do we have value to offer (service, experience, perspective they need)?

Using this criteria, go through the attendee list if the event publishes it, and if they don't, they likely published last year's attendee list and that's ok. Making some assumptions here, if they attended last year, the odds are good they'll attend this year as well so use that list. Often- times for larger events/shows there is a portal in the show site which allows you to e-mail the company/person/brand. If this exists, use it. If not, be creative on how you can connect with them. The likelihood that you already have the name and contact information for this prospect is good given the work you've already done preparing your outbound target data base. If there is not any listing of attendees, either for the upcoming event or for last year's session, that's ok. Go directly to your target database, comb through it, determine which of your targets might be attending and send them a note. Two things happen here:

1. If they are planning to attend they now know you are involved in their industry to the degree that you would be attending their event and that speaks to your expertise.
2. If they are not planning to attend for some reason, they are likely impressed that you will be and if they take the time to let you know they will not be attending, be sure to let them know you'll be happy to give them a summary of the highlights upon your

return. *Btw: this is also a reminder to include any post event summary and insight sharing as an outbound e-mail to your entire targeted data base.*

Now that we have identified those we want to connect with prior to the event, it's time to reach out and introduce you and your agency to them, let them know you will be attending and would like to meet them. Remember, the goal here is introduction, not promotion..... there is time for that later. For now, we want to make an e-mail introduction to them and ask if we may meet in person for a proper introduction. Now don't be discouraged if you don't get a reply on this first mailing, remember they are busy getting ready and setting up their own appointments. Regardless if you get a response or not, they have now been soft introduced to you so if you do meet them it's not a blind introduction. I typically do not get many responses on the first outreach, yet do on the next one which is where we make a plan to meet either in their booth or somewhere else at the event.

The other detail you want to be thinking through is how you'll spend your time at the event. Which breakouts you will attend, which networking parties to attend, which training seminars to attend and where to place yourself during transition times and evening times. The goal is to invite or be invited to mini events like dinner, cocktails, coffee, etc. with your prospects, but this is not always possible. *One tip here. If this event is sponsored by a media outlet and you happen to place a lot of media in their outlets, don't be shy to ask your rep to set up a dinner with some of your top prospects. Remember, your rep would love for you to have these prospects as clients, and of course their media budgets through your agency.*

If you are attending a large trade show take a moment and map out your path and be sure you know where all your prospect booths are located so you don't miss them or run out of time to connect. As you make your plan, you know who you want to meet, you've sent out invitations to connect, you have arranged diners with a few prospects, etc. be sure you have something of value to say to them. Not to worry, you are on top of the conversation of the vertical, and you've been publishing white papers and podcasts on a variety of relevant content so you have plenty to choose from, just be sure you can bring the topic around to their company, brand and business.

Case Study Development

Another key tool in the prospecting tool box is relevant case studies for sharing. Just like the use of white papers on the topics we publish are a deeper dive on our perspective on the topic, case studies are proof we know what to do with the insights and information. Now, there are a wide variety of case study formats (I'm pretty sure I've used them all by the way) and there is no right or wrong way to do it. That said, I would suggest that you ere on the side of brevity when preparing your case studies for use in the context of business development follow up. These case studies are not necessarily the same ones you include in a formal RFI or RFP response or versions you might use during a live pitch, these are one more tool you are pulling out of the tool box to help secure an in-person meeting (or phone introduction at the very least). Consider it a proof point that the topic being discussed and the problem/opportunity you solved for is something you have experience in. The irony of this is not lost on me here. We have been so focused on positioning our expertise and indeed elevating our experiences to expertise that we now are seemingly going backwards to prove we can do it. Consider this for a moment, would you rather be tasked with convincing a prospect you CAN do the work or that you HAVE done the work? Positioning your agency as an expert in the field is the highest value point on the decision making journey your prospect will engage in. Said another way, If the prospect believes you have done similar work, yet does not believe you are as experienced and expert in their business, you are likely being invited in to execute their plan or thinking. If, on the other hand, they have been intrigued by your thinking and level of expertise/perspective on their business vertical, they are accepting an invitation to partner at a higher strategic level. This is Maslow at its finest. Value lies in the partnership relationships, not the vendor relationships. Where do you want to start?

In the end, prospecting is what you make of it. If you believe you can load up your CRM and automate responses to inquiries like it's a product lead nurture, you will be frustrated and ultimately disappointed with the results. If, on the other hand, you recognize that the inbound/outbound efforts are only one point in the overall business development process, you will be better for it and frankly more successful filling and converting your new business pipeline. The prospecting efforts of an agency, regardless of the type or the size, include a strong understanding of the business of your prospect's business, an ability to communicate your value proposition to that audience and a way to reach them and track their response. Remember, the initial step in getting more clients is making an introduction. The question is what type of introduction do you want to make, what will you say and how will you know they heard you? These are all questions we should be asking ourselves as we engage in preparing our business development plan which includes the ultimate payoff of new client business. Remember, services are bought, not sold so we must be there, top of mind, when a prospect has a need.

CHAPTER 8

NEW BUSINESS VS BUSINESS DEVELOPMENT

I like to say that business development is what we do for our clients every day and that doing it for our own agency is really no different. The efforts we put forth on their behalf are philosophically the same efforts we need to engage in for ourselves.

Almost everyone I meet in the agency business who does not have a formalized business development strategy in place will refer to the effort as New Business or Sales. I'm always struck by this because it seems that these are generally very smart folks who are held in high regard by their clients for helping them grow and expand their markets, yet they are short sighted on this topic when it comes to their own business. For fun, I'm going to share some quotes I've heard over the years that will probably ring true with many of you. If any of these do, don't worry, you are in good company. This is how many refer to the need to expand/grow their business:

1. I need someone to do new business for me.
2. I just need a good sales person to go get us some more clients.
3. If I had more time, I could go get us new clients myself.

4. I don't have to do new business because we get calls all the time for work.
5. My new business comes to me .

I'd like to suggest for a moment that new business is one of four key business development growth pillars. For the reasons we have gone over thus far in this book, we understand that getting a new client is not all it takes to grow. It takes keeping your current clients engaged and seeing value in what you deliver, it takes having folks ready and confident to do the work, it takes leveraging that great work in the industries you serve to make sure the awareness of your expertise is being seen by your prospects and it takes year after year of self-regulating your service and value offering to maintain the positive growth trajectory you are on. If not, your agency will resemble the stock market during the early days of the COVID-19 pandemic, with huge peaks and valleys and a seemingly revolving door of talent and client brands.

The difference between new business and business development is apparent if we take a moment and think about what goes into each. We can say that all business development plans include new business, however not all new business plans include a broader business development plan. This is why we see so many agencies who seemingly win clients (for a while) fail to grow. It's because they are churning, which is very expensive and not to mention frustrating. Take a look at this basic growth platform model. Are you thinking of your business this way?

Growth Platforms

AT THE CORE OF ANY GROWTH STRATEGY

EXISTING CLIENTS

Maintain
Grow
Expand

NEW BUSINESS

Expertise Vertical
Strategic Adjacencies

TRAINING

Functional
Expertise

INDUSTRY

Integrate
Get Involved

If we apply our Assess, Prepare, Prospect approach to these four growth platforms we are likely to find ourselves in the type of pitches we want to be invited to and with a better than average chance of winning. The truth is, there is a cadence to an agencies growth trajectory that treats each of these pillars as equal growth platforms. This cadence can go either direction, and when it flows as shown below, we see year after year of iterative growth. If, however, the flow is reversed we see what I affectionately refer to as the "death spiral" of an agency. Let's keep the momentum going in the right direction, and when we do that it looks something like this:

Growth Trajectory

YOU'RE EITHER GREEN AND GROWING OR RIPE AND ROTING

CURRENT CLIENTS

Maintain
Grow
Expand

NEW BUSINESS

Expertise Vertical
Strategic Adjacencies

TRAINING

Functional
Expertise

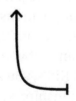

INDUSTRY

Integrate
Get Involved

Existing Clients

Looking into these four growth platforms there are certain strategies to consider for each. Let's begin with our existing clients. We've talked about how important it is to keep our existing clients satisfied and seeing value in what we have to offer, yet we have not broken this down until now. If we take a look at the three strategies under this growth platform we see that we must first maintain, then grow, then expand. Let's dive into that.

Maintaining existing clients will draw from two other growth platforms: Training and Industry Involvement. You can see now why I consider this grouping of growth platforms overlaid onto the Assess, Prepare, Prospect approach as a tightly integrated business development approach. To maintain good standing with our current clients we know we must not only deliver on what has been agreed to (project or agency of record scope of work), we must also bring new thinking to them (as outlined in the Prepare chapter under Initiative Thinking). To do this we will need a staff of trained and confident associates who are conversant and fluid in understanding the business of their business. It's one thing to execute a book of work, it's a whole other to partner with the client to help them traverse their given landscape in a way that positions them to grow or survive depending on their market conditions. Regardless of their current market dynamics, if your agency is seen as adding value to the identified KPI's, you are more likely to see another year of the relationship. Never take for granted the tenure of your relationship, they are all vulnerable to some degree.

Another aspect of maintaining your current clients includes how well you integrate into the conversation of their industry with them. This industry involvement with them can take on many forms, not the least of which includes how your agency partners with them to achieve higher than expected results from the industry events they participate in such as trade shows, conferences, associations, etc. Also worth considering is partnering with them in going to market with insights on their customers/consumers which the industry as a whole will see value in. This definitely helps solidify your relationship while giving your agency the exposure in a light you can benefit from with prospects for yourself. So, you see, these growth platforms are integrated and interconnective. They do not stand alone, even when we are considering the strategies to engage to keep the clients we have.

Growing existing clients in the simplest form can be achieved one of two ways.

1. Bring new services to existing client work
2. Bring existing services to new client work

Nothing earth shattering here, however it is often overlooked or taken for granted that our existing clients know and understand everything we do. Don't be so sure. I'm known for my response when folks tell me that the client they've had for 10 years "knows exactly who they are and what they have to offer" (picture a snarky look as this is delivered). What I usually say at this point is "the client knows the 10 year old version of who you are and that may not include the new services you've adopted over the past 3 years" and follow up by inquiring how many of the new services they've adopted or created over the past few years are being purchased by this client. Furthermore, if they have not created any new services or introduced new services for this client are they still seeing the value and margin of the 10 year old services they do engage with them on? in some cases they do and they are still making money, however, moreover they are not. This is where I point back to our talent and service audit to assess where the opportunities are with this particular client and to determine which, if any, of the new services we offer other clients make sense for this particular client.

An appropriate time to make sure your current clients know about any new services you are offering is during the annual or better yet, semi-annual business review. I always like to include a section at the end of each business review that includes where we've innovated since we last reviewed the business and usually includes new services, new acquisitions, new association memberships, etc. This is one way to ensure your clients know the current version of your agency and what you have to offer. If you don't currently conduct formal business reviews with your clients, I highly recommend you do. It's important to ensure you are keeping the relationship strong and valuable.

Expanding existing clients has more to do with division and/or location expansion than service expansion we just addressed. Take a moment and look at your current client and consider which other divisions, locations, brands, etc. you may have "permission to win" with. If you determine that there are indeed other divisions, locations, brands, etc. you believe you have services they can benefit from, then don't be shy asking your current contact to introduce you to those other opportunity areas. Expanding into additional divisions and/or locations makes you even more "sticky" with that client not to mention more informed and better positioned to add value. We have talked about bringing initiatives to existing clients; well this includes initiatives that cross divisions. Think of a cross promotions, sales/marketing integration or divisional partnering on a new product or service launch, etc. You get the picture. This expansion inside existing clients can also mean adding additional brands under the corporate banner. Consider for a moment how many individual brands reside under the General Mills banner and you can see that the opportunity is grand. Again, I'd not be shy about asking your current client on brand X, whom is completely impressed with you and your agency by the way, to help you penetrate some of these other brands. The other thing to consider here is that many brand directors have a stable of brands they are responsible for and thus, it makes sense that you work on all of them under their responsibility. Which brings me to another very important point to cover under the topic of existing clients and that is to constantly be working towards building relationships as high up in the client organization as you can. Easy to say, harder to do sometimes. Let's be honest, many times the brand shepherds we work with do not want to introduce us around the company, so to speak, for fear of having our attention becoming fractured. The solve? Create a platform to share (go to your conversation audit for topic inspiration) which more than the current brand can benefit from. Open up this sharing summit to others in their company. Honestly, your current client brand partner should be interested in facilitating this summit because the light will shine favorably on them as well for having such an integrated agency partner on their team who's willing and able to share such valuable knowledge. Try it.

Another way to expand is into additional markets or through continued franchising by your current client. There are such a variety of services one can offer to their current client if they are willing to invest in the work to become experienced and ultimately an expert, in the elements of an expansion plan which include new market development. Consider, for a moment, the need for LSM around a newly franchised restaurant chain. Those needs, while strategically aligned regardless of the new market, will differ for each tactical execution. Creating an area of expertise around the ability to help establish, promote and drive traffic to a new franchisee location for a restaurant chain is something that has real opportunity. The theory holds for all kinds of franchised business models from restaurants to hotels, to banks, to cellular companies and muffler shops.

CHAPTER 9

NEW BUSINESS

While this is where many start the conversation around growth, it's merely one of four growth pillars we need to look at. The reality is that while maintaining our current clients must be job #1, new business is right behind it.

Now, not all new business opportunity is created the same. For example, there are new business opportunities that find us which we have no business engaging in, yet we do. There are others we pursue for literally years, before we have a shot at gaining, and we do this as well. The chasm in between these two scenarios is the broad field of play for new business, and one which, if not navigated strategically, can eat an agency alive and leave it for the vultures. Think of Mad Max and all the crazy opponents on that battlefield; things we could never describe as our competitive set coming at us with a fury, and we didn't even know they exist. That's what the field of new business can feel like if we don't calibrate our expectations and actions. I tend to categorize new business into two categories of opportunity:

- Our Expertise Vertical(s)
- Strategic Adjacencies

The business verticals in which we can profess some level of expertise, or at least experience when we are starting out, is where to begin. It's where we have "permission to win" and so that's where we will prospect. Recall that Indian motorcycle story I shared earlier in the book. That is exactly why we must be strategic about where we spend our time, energy, gifts and investments prospecting if we are going to gain the right new clients and work. Gaining new business should not, and frankly cannot, be a losing proposition. For if it is, it's not new business, it's new expense, isn't it? I mention this because while absurd to think we will spend money to gain bad business and then lose money managing it, we do. We do because by nature most agency folks are hardcore competitors and the type of competitors which will not go quietly into the night. No, we fight, push, cajole and stick with it because we believe we can make any client a good client. The reality is not all clients are good for us, they may not be a bad client, they may just be a bad client for us. So how do we mitigate getting engaged and even married to bad clients? Well that is where my two simple categories of new clients comes in. This first category, clients who are in the business verticals where we have "permission to win," is where we begin. Regardless of the vertical/category, there are likely enough non-competing brands/companies inside that vertical to keep us as busy as we want to be. Just consider the prospecting list you have created from the direction in the Preparation section of the book and you'll be convinced of that. The criteria we use to describe our perfect client is our guide and will be the barometer by which we measure any engagement regardless of how we find ourselves in conversation with them. Remember, we thought long and hard about the type of client we want to have and whom we can service most efficiently and effectively. Don't stop following those guidelines just because we are in a new business hunt. In fact, even more the reason to adhere to our principals while engaged in the hunt.

The power of saying no to an invitation is liberating. Now, I'm a realist, and agree that if someone wants us to pursue a working relationship with them and we don't have any idea what the real KPI's or goals of the industry they work in revolve around, yet want to spend a lot of advertising funds with us, I'm going to have to think hard before passing on it. I will, however, not miss the opportunity to be transparent with the unlikely suiter and let them know where our value resides in such an engagement. If, on the other hand, we bracket our prospecting as described earlier, and we do in fact attract the right type of new client prospect, then we must do all we can to win them over and that includes engaging right away in helping them navigate the landscape of that vertical.

When engaging inside our focused vertical and actively pursuing clients that we have "permission to win" with, don't be shy about sharing the stories (case studies) of your past success. And if you find yourself with specific category expertise inside this business vertical and no client to share it with, start there. What I mean is this, we don't keep clients forever, even if it feels like it sometimes, and when a client does leave us for whatever reason, don't let that expertise go to waste. The insights and expertise around a specific category inside the business vertical is perishable, it has a shelf life of value. Generally speaking, if you are not working inside a category for more than 18 months, you are likely a bit out of touch with the trends and key drivers and can use some brushing up. Consider for a moment that your focused vertical is the foodservice vertical and your clients are the food and beverage manufacturers that supply the food distributors and restaurant communities. If you have had a client in the poultry category of foodservice for the past 10 years and for whatever reason you have parted ways, you have an 18 month window where you can confidently approach all the other poultry providers in that vertical with real and relevant perspectives on their business, the poultry business inside the foodservice vertical. So, start there. This goes for any category inside your focused vertical. As part of your partner level work with this past poultry provider inside the foodservice vertical you are well aware of the competitive set you had to navigate on their behalf. Well, once you and said poultry provider parted ways, every one of those then competitors just became your top prospects. The Replacement Strategy is one that I love to engage in on behalf of the clients I work with because it's as if we have just been released from solving one brand's challenges inside a very deliberate and finite arena and are now at liberty to take all that intelligence and insight that we garnered by digging deep into a category for our old client and we are bursting at the seams to apply that to a new brand. There is something intoxicating about knocking on the door of a brand with an insight/perspective you feel so strongly can help them achieve a variety of goals that drives this Replacement Strategy. So, don't let any grass grow under your relevance, so to speak. Once you know you will be parting ways with a client in a particular category, start immediately identifying your new target prospects to replace them. As you can imagine, what you have to share will be very interesting to the rest of the competitive set in that category. So, when it comes to hunting new business inside your focused vertical, begin with categories inside that vertical where you have "permission to win," and if you've recently ended a client relationship, start with that category. Leveraging category insights is not the same as leveraging brand insights so don't shy away from your newly departed clients' competition. They'll be happy to talk to you. You can rest easy knowing you will not be divulging brand secrets, rather category insights.

When it comes to expanding your reach beyond your current focused vertical there is no need to throw strategy out the window and begin soliciting any brand/client in any vertical. No, instead, dissect your USP and value proposition to uncover transferable and relevant equites of those which can translate to strategically adjacent verticals. What I mean by this is that just because we work with restaurants does not mean we cannot work with muffler shops. Let me explain. Let's assume you work with quick service and fast casual restaurant chains in the areas of franchise communications, promotion, menu innovation, menu launch, media, etc. One might say that what you do for these restaurant clients is help them grow through market and franchise expansion. There is much to consider when we work with franchisors and franchisees and that way of working is transferable to a variety of verticals predicated on that type of business model. So, consider that while you may work with restaurants, what you truly understand is how to navigate the landscape created by a franchisor/franchisee environment. Now that has real value to anyone in that business model scenario.

One of the most valuable and eye opening exercises I lead clients through is helping them determine what other adjacent strategic verticals they have "permission to win" in. Consider a model I use for this exercise.

The Core in this model is your current focused vertical, the Selling Proposition can be considered "what you do for that vertical" and the Strategic Adjacencies are other verticals where that particular selling proposition has value.

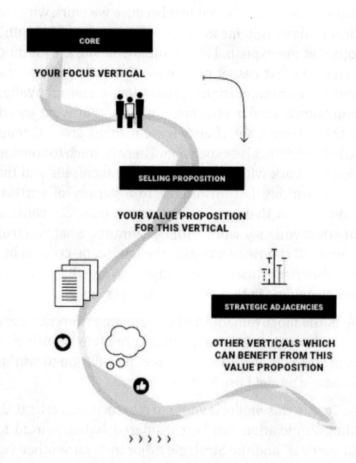

Strategic Adjacencies

LEVERAGE YOUR UNIQUE SELLING PROPOSITION

CORE

YOUR FOCUS VERTICAL

SELLING PROPOSITION

YOUR VALUE PROPOSITION FOR THIS VERTICAL

STRATEGIC ADJACENCIES

OTHER VERTICALS WHICH CAN BENEFIT FROM THIS VALUE PROPOSITION

Core---------Selling Proposition--------Strategic Adjacencies

Transportation:	We elevate the value of the Franchisor to the Franchisee	QSR, Fast Casual, Family Dine, Repair Shops
	We understand Traveler Insights	Train, Airline, Car Rental, Tour Operator, Cruise line

Now, viable strategic adjacencies that are available to an agency can be very close in and intuitive or indeed, less intuitive and further outside what you may initially expect. So, consider your USP and what you currently "do" for your clients today and do it in a way that allows you to deconstruct your proposition and identify which aspects of its current client value are transferable to other adjacent verticals. If you work in the foodservice vertical, are you viable and valuable in the agriculture or ingredient vertical? If you are focused on the automotive industry are you believable and viable in the automotive aftermarket retail space? If you're centered on healthcare/hospital are you valuable to the those brands in the pharmaceutical industry? Know your true value, know the real insight and knowledge you have relative to the clients you serve today and simply dissect those out of your USP to see where else they can apply. This is a fascinating exercise and one which will leave you feeling optimistic about your growth path.

Chapter 10

Training

Training in general is often overlooked inside agencies. It's not that folks don't see the value in it, it's just something no one usually wants to tackle. I've heard so many reasons why agencies don't formally take on training and the implications to their sustainability shows. Some of the reasons I've heard why they don't formalize their training include a lot of the usual suspects such as:

- I don't have anyone I can spare to head that up.
- We are doing just fine with the way things are going right now. I don't need to make the investment in training.
- If I train them they'll just leave and take all this insight with them and I'll have to start all over again.
- Training is something they need to pick up on their own. No one trained me and I was better for it.
- Training around here looks like paying attention and being curious. We pride ourselves on that.
- Etc.

So, while the entire notion of training is misunderstood and often overlooked, it is not without impact to the business. An untrained staff will leave the principals doing all the heavy lifting, it will leave the staff insecure of their ability to grow and it will cheat the clients of the best the agency has to offer. That said, if you are an agency that believes in training and do your best to provide the most valuable training for your team, I commend you. Now consider imagining your training regimen through the lens of business development and see how you might adjust your effort.

Training as part of the business development conversation sometimes has folks questioning if I have this growth platform in the right place. I do. Consider what training means if it falls under HR or Account Service or Insights, or any other department or discipline inside an agency. It tends to become one dimensional and territorial. I am suggesting that we look at training as an integral part of the overall business development growth effort and as such, focus not only on the functional aspects of the agency, but also on the focused verticals we have chosen to work in. Helping your team understand the business of your client's business will help build an army of experts at each level in the agency, and your clients and your chosen industry vertical, will stand up and take notice. You will become that expert agency in the areas you focus on. Not a bad reputation to have.

Training Approach

The value of training at the agency level goes far beyond the personal knowledge each recipient gains. Consider for a moment the effect a well-educated team has on the following:

- Ability to diversify bench strength on client teams
- Driven experts trained in "our" way of thinking
- Number of capable ambassadors ready to explore our focused verticals
- Confidence of team to interact on a higher intellectual level with potential clients

- Recruiting message
- Client retention value
- Client training venue/value add
- Readiness for growth
- Expectation setting: Expect Expertise
- Common language and consistent messaging
- Cultural swagger
- Industry reputation
- Content for outbound and perspectives
- Client pioneering
- And so many more.......

These, and others, are why a well thought through and executed Agency Training program is so vital to the growth and stability of the shop.

There are two key focus areas of training to consider:

1. Functional aspects of what it takes to produce work at an agency.
2. Expertise: the aspects of your clients business and industry that everyone on the team needs to understand to be able to add value through their functional contribution.

What's really interesting about the two key focus areas of training that I've dealt with over the years is the push back from certain departments and/or disciplines inside the agency and their questioning of "why" they need to know this or that to the degree that other areas or disciplines need to. Imagine if you can, an art director who believes they don't really need to understand the intricacies of a particular channel they are being asked to concept for because, "it's stifling to their creativity and the creative process" (I've actually heard this one). Now imagine what would happen if that same art director was to manage a photo or video shoot and leave out, or worse, keep in, aspects of the environment that would let everyone know they do not understand the category, the target or the problem they are trying to solve. Well, I can tell you, the client who "trusted us" to make sure what we were doing would position them in the best light with the target we were going after would be seen as irrelevant and not in tune with the industry and the customer. Likewise, the other agency prospects out in the industry would recognize this is a poor showing for that particular brand, which can ultimately get back to your agency as the one who produced it. Not good. So, you see, because everything communicates, everyone on the team must be engaged at the same level of expertise to ensure the full deliverable is on mark, relevant and insightful. No one should be able to play the "not my role" card when it comes to industry expertise training.

So, where to begin? Here is one possible approach/structure to consider:

A. Identifying the top 10-12 courses you need to kick the effort off with. Consider:

    a. Agency economics 101 (how we make money)

    b. Strategic Selling

    c. How to work a trade show

    d. How to find THE insight

    e. How to write an effective creative brief

    f. Client Relations

    g. Industry Specific training geared to your areas of expertise/your vertical

    h. Etc.

B. Identify the new areas we must learn and begin to incorporate into our daily client work to stay relevant and seen as a value. There is likely a Value Audit that should be conducted at some point to better identify what your clients value and not what we *think* they value. The gap here is often astounding and informative.

   a. Identify senior people in the agency to learn these areas, prepare a training module and teach it.

C. Identify our "professors", our teachers of the modules. This can range from senior folks for topics such as Strategic Selling or Working a Trade Show, down to entry levels for channel and category deep dives such as: The role SEO or motion is playing in your focused channels/verticals.

D. Challenge the professor to understand where we fit into the topic conversation or/and where we can "jump in" with a leading perspective. These perspectives are perishable so they are short lived modules but should always have a slot in the curriculum.

E. Align internally on topics and professors (remember, not all classes need to be taught by our own people, invite outside guests to speak as well).

F. Align internally on the name of your program and branding of it (we are agencies after all) and create certificates and/or some way of recognizing each course completed.

G. Calendar out the entire "semester" with class descriptors, dates, locations, length of class and professor.

H. Hold an "open enrollment" lunch and learn whereby the agency, and whomever you want to invite to participate (think clients), can mingle among the professors, see the classes and ideally the venue for the classes. Have the following information available by which to choose their classes:

   a. Class title and brief description of the topic and why it is important

   b. Professor teaching it and a short bio

   c. Dates/times offered

   d. Sign-up sheet with known maximum allowed

   e. Comments from the professor: what you can expect to learn

I. Integrate the participation and teaching into individual associate performance assessment and possibly the bonus program (need to demonstrate this is a serious aspect and catalyst to our growth)

J. Be prepared to film these classes for future use and remote access

K. Creating the library of modules produced and making sure they stay relevant and updated (this is a long term tactic)

L. Institute and organize "Ride Alongs" in our core focus areas/channels/verticals to ensure reality based/hands on learning opportunities as well

M. Consider tapping into your local university to request class and lab audits

N. Encourage cross functional training in house. We can cross train our own folks.

O. Inspiration training and how to find what builds a person's fire for growth. These are often more "excursion" based modules such as a Go-Find or scavenger hunt style class with pointed outcomes expected.

Industry Integration/Involvement

So, where to begin? How about the beginning? There is seemingly an association for almost anything you can imagine. Mushrooms? Yup. In fact, there are 80,000 results in Google for the search, <u>Mushroom Associations</u>. So, if you are wondering if the vertical you are focused in, or want to focus in, has an association, the answer is likely YES. So start there. The value of beginning your search for ways to get involved by checking out he association is because they are likely the most objective perspective you are going to get on the industry itself. If we consider for a moment the objective or mission of most associations, it becomes clear that they are in the business of providing real and relevant information/insights to those who are members or followers. The association is the place to identify the most important conversations happening in that vertical and likely they will host or sponsor or promote an annual convention or summit to help bring everyone together to discuss the topics prevailing in the conversation.

A good place to begin your industry integration and involvement is to make a list of the top 3-5 events taking place in the focused vertical of your choice and visit the websites promoting those events to understand what you can expect by attending. I always like to see who the event organizer suggests attend because that is telling as to what type of client prospects I can expect to find there if I choose to attend. Remember, just because it's the biggest event in the industry, it may be attended by folks who are not in a position to engage you as an agency, and so, perhaps you go to the #2 event in the industry and so on. If, however, the biggest event in the industry is the best place to learn more about the issues, opportunities and trends of that industry, it's likely worth an "audit" by you or your team to learn the intricacies' of the conversation happening. Auditing your first ever attendance to the big industry event should be with eyes wide open and note taking in mind. Consider that most of the folks attending this particular big event have likely been attending for many years and may have lost their ability to see the news or be objective about the conversation; something to do with being jaded or closed minded (I personally attended over 20 National Restaurant Association shows and they all started to seem the same to me.) There is value in new perspective and there is insight to share when we can observe objectively and see new opportunities others may not.

You may be well indoctrinated into the industry you serve and thus, know the shows, events, the conversations and the opportunities at hand. For you, the next step is becoming more integrated with the governing arms of the industry and those that shape the narrative. That includes the events, shows and conventions but it also includes the deeper insights uncovered by real research and objective perspectives. One of the best ways to make it to the center stage/keynote slot at these events is to have something unique to share that everyone else can benefit from. Duh, right? While this may be a simple concept to grasp, it's often assumed that as agency folks we don't have permission to be the author and orator of this insight..... we do. In fact, oftentimes we are the only ones involved in the event, show or association that has a truly unbiased perspective on the situation and thus, the most objective insights to share. So, get involved, dig for new insights, write, speak and share your thoughts with the industry organizers and be the voice that is leading the evolution of the conversation. It matters.

Parting Thoughts

You have your Permission to Win, it's always been with you, you just have to unlock it, feed it, nurture it, encourage it and be courageous in your pursuit of strategic growth.

Build your agency by demonstrating Trust and Respect while Expecting Expertise from everyone on the team. Be curious and push yourself to learn a new thing, willingly throw yourself into uncomfortable situations and scenarios that make you stretch.

Include innovation and pioneering into your vernacular, live into a "lean forward" posture filled with grace and grit for learning through trial.

Learn to say NO to the seemingly easy way and YES to the challenges.

Be an encourager not a just a promotor. Lead with confidence and transparency to your humanity.

Collaborate not commiserate. Make decisions, take action, monitor, measure and adjust.

Probably the most important of all, and that which can help us wake up every day and do this crazy thing we do, is to remember that we have a choice when it comes to how we build our business and that decision is up to you. It all starts with you.

Cheers
DVA

CPSIA information can be obtained
at www.ICGtesting.com
Printed in the USA
BVHW052214080421
604476BV00006B/1607